CRISTIE KERR
A Great American Golfer

A Father's Story

CRISTIE KERR
A Great American Golfer
A Father's Story

Written by Michael Kerr
With Dr. Barbara W. Moller-Kerr

©2010 Michael Kerr

All Rights Reserved

No part of this book may be reproduced or distributed in any form, including photocopying, electronic or mechanical means, or through any type of information storage or retrieval systems, without permission in writing from the author or publisher of this book, except for the minimum number of words needed for review.

Cover Photo by JLBarranco
via iStockPhoto.com

Cover & Interior Layout by
EditWriteDesign.com

CRISTIE KERR
A Father's Story

PREFACE

Michael Kerr has captured the essence of the development of a golfer from puberty to maturity and the heights of professional stardom. Michael and Linda Kerr made numerous sacrifices for Cristie, but without Cristie's desire, dedication and untold hours of practice and tournament play, she could not have reached her place in professional golf stardom. I congratulate Michael on his book's portrayal of the trials and tribulations of a junior golfer, and Linda Kerr's unwavering support, for the professional achievements made by Cristie. I'm proud to have been a part of Cristie's life and her development.

~ Charlie DeLucca, Dade Amateur Golf Association

INTRODUCTION

Have you ever wondered why some parents devote all their spare time, income, and family savings to help their child learn to play a sport with the hope that the child will excel, perhaps even become famous? Some parents do this because their young child exhibits an unusual athletic gift. Others rationalize that it's a great way to spend quality time with their child, and some want to give their child the opportunity that they themselves never had, or were denied. My story about Cristie Kerr and how she became a great American golfer is a combination of all these motivations.

Cristie's mother Linda and I nurtured and encouraged our talented child to help her pursue a dream. While all parents dream about their child doing something special in life, our dream became Cristie's. This journey from childhood to stardom was fueled with help from many people. It is not easy being a parent, coach, manager, driver, travel agent, caddy, and fan, but the journey to professional athletics involved all of these roles and more. Helping Cristie to succeed required numerous difficult choices and sacrifices from Cristie, her mother and me, as well as numerous other family members and friends. Everyone played an important role in her success.

Not all children who show promise will reach the professional level in their sport. Some will quit, not willing to put forth the required effort, and some families will not be able to provide the needed financial resources. In some cases injuries will prevent athletes from following their dream. Success requires an arduous process over many years and in some cases, decades. It is not an overnight accomplishment. No short cuts can speed up the process. Hard work, dedication and the desire to achieve are the ingredients of a winner.

I do not imagine that any parent who reads this story will turn to his child and say, "Okay, let's get started, you're going to learn how to play golf and become a professional golfer." I hope that my story will help readers develop an understanding of the obstacles that Cristie had to overcome and how many people in her life helped her become one of golf's superstars.

I grew up dreaming of playing professional baseball. A typical boy, I loved playing games outdoors with my friends. Almost every day we played stickball against the school wall. I would hit the ball as hard as I could so I could watch my friends move back near the fence to try to catch the ball. They hated climbing over the fence to retrieve the home runs I hit.

My dad was very athletic and loved to play handball with his brothers. On Sundays, at Brighton Beach in Coney Island, Brooklyn, they played handball, and I watched. How I longed to be part of the game rather than just sitting in the hot sun as a spectator, but I was not allowed to play, because this was "a man's game," and no kids were allowed.

As a ninth grader in high school, I tried out for the football and baseball teams. I made the junior varsity football and varsity baseball teams. I played in both, but I was a starter on the baseball team. When I was in tenth grade, I competed against juniors and seniors on the baseball team for a starting position, and I became a starting player, hitting in the cleanup forth spot, since I was the power hitter.

Our baseball coach was called "Pops," because to the team he appeared very old, probably around fifty. During preseason games, Pops saw that I could drive the baseball over the outfielder's head and hit hard line drives and ground balls that were difficult to catch. With my strong throwing arm, I played right field, since I could throw runners out at third base and home plate.

Things were going well for me as a high school athlete until one day after a junior varsity football game, I walked into my home, and my mother took one look at me and started to scream. Apparently, I had been hit in the face during the game, and looked pretty bad. I did not feel any pain; in fact, I was not even aware that I was injured until I looked in the mirror. One eye was black and blue and almost closed, my lips were cut, and my nose was bruised and bleeding.

My mother screamed to my father, "Tell him he can't play football anymore!" I argued with her and cried. I did just about everything to convince her to allow me to play on the team, but she was determined that my football days were over. The next day, my overly protective mother stormed into the principal's office and demanded that I be taken off the football team. She hated sports and was determined to make sure that her son was not going to be scarred or disfigured for life from football.

Her actions embarrassed me and made me angry. I resented what she had done, but I had no choice. In those days I followed my mother's edicts, no questions asked! My coach tried to reason with her, but he could not change her decision. The principal would not override her either. Because I felt that my mother was being unreasonable, I was devastated and determined that I would not let her do this to me in baseball.

Baseball was my best sport. I led the team and league in batting average and home runs. By the end of my senior year, just as the baseball season was coming to an end, the coach said, "Mike, at some of the games professional baseball scouts are looking at you to possibly play minor league baseball." Describing the living conditions for minor league players and how little money they earn, the coach reminded me that some players never get to the majors and play their entire career in the minor leagues. Other players, who never make it, quit to work other jobs. While the coach believed that I had the ability and potential, he cautioned that there was no guarantee that I would make it to the majors. I wanted the opportunity to try. Playing professional baseball was my dream.

Excited about the chance to pursue my dream of playing professional baseball, I told my dad what I had discussed with my coach. Because my father did not want to disagree or argue with my mother, he responded, "Speak to your mother, if she says it's all right, then it is all right with me." Mom's answer was what I dreaded, a definitive "NO!" She demanded that I give up the ridiculous dream of playing baseball and go to college. I never forgot that day and was determined that when I became a parent I would never do to my child what my mother had done to me. I would give my kid every opportunity to pursue a dream, no matter what it might be. Today many years later, I look back at the disappointment I felt due to my mom's attitude; but now I thank her, because had she not taken that approach with me, I might not have done what I did for my daughter, Cristie Kerr.

A Father's Story

This story of how Cristie became a great American golfer began as a journal, which I kept for twelve years after she showed an interest in golf. This book is for readers who are interested in her life's story and how Cristie became one of the great female golfers of modern time. Parents who have a child with athletic ability or those who know a child is interested in a competitive sport may find my story a valuable resource to understand the commitment and obstacles Cristie, her mother, and I had to overcome. This story describes Cristie's exposure to a variety of sports and why she decided to concentrate solely on golf. Her struggles and accomplishments are revealed as she worked to earn her place in golf's history books.

This story is told from notes in my journal as well as my memory. Some family members or friends may recall some incidents in a different way, but my hope is that this story will help other parents understand what it takes to provide their child with an opportunity to do something special that most children never accomplish. My journey with Cristie on the road to becoming a professional golfer was some of the most exciting years of my life.

Cristie Kerr

A Father's Story

CHAPTER ONE
Discovering Young Talent

Most parents wonder what it is like to discover great talent or "genius" in a child. When a new baby is held by the loving family, many dreams and aspirations go through the minds of the parents, grandparents, siblings, and adoring family friends. They wonder, "Could this be the next president, the author of a great novel, a movie star, a world famous athlete, an artist, or a great inventor?" The list goes on and on of the dreams for our children, those we discuss, and those we hold in our hearts. All families dream, so how do some dreams become reality? A common image of a prodigy is very young child sitting at a piano playing beautiful, complicated music. Another common image is a toddler who reads and loves to discuss the exciting ideas in books, long before his school mates will encounter these passages. Very young children also have demonstrated unusual ability to paint or work in the arts. How does it happen?

One of the first elements in any of these stories is exposure. The child prodigy at the piano obviously had access to a piano and probably had a great deal of exposure to one or more persons playing the piano very well. Children who read early are surrounded by books and people who read aloud and share the pleasure of the printed word. The young artist often has a playroom which includes art supplies with parents who are creative and who praise early artistic efforts.

An early start on the road to success in sports, particularly individual competitive sports, requires exposure at a young age. Watching television with a child will not generate the interest that comes from participating in family sports or attending local athletic activities. Sports are a natural interest for many children, who enjoy being active and having fun. Even a preschool child, who does not have the coordination or strength to engage in many sports, can still watch family members and imitate activities that are within their ability to execute.

Cristie watched her mother and me enjoy a variety of sports. At seven years old, Cristie spent three or four nights a week watching us play tennis, retrieving tennis balls, and bringing towels and drinks. Soon Cristie wanted to learn how to hit tennis balls, even if the large, heavy racket was too difficult for her to swing and hit the ball over the net.

The Miami summer weather is hot and humid even at night, which made playing tennis uncomfortable. Looking for recreational that was less exhausting in the heat, her mother and I began bowling with the adult bowling leagues at the Don Carter Lanes near our home. Soon we were spending three to four nights a week bowling in different leagues, which provided socialization with people of all ages in the comfort of an air-conditioned bowling alley, with a place to eat and drink.

Initially, Cristie played video arcade games while we bowled, but before long she wanted to learn to bowl. Lessons were arranged, and as she improved, we bought her a custom fitted ball and bowling shoes. Cristie enjoyed bowling, especially since she could run over to the arcade, play a quick video game before her turn to bowl or run to the restaurant to get something to eat or drink.

After only a few months of lessons, Cristie was bowling scores from 100 to 140. By the time she was eight, she was carrying a bowling average of 140, which is quite impressive for an adult, but even more impressive for a kid. The bowling alley had a children's league, where Cristie and three other girls—all named Cristie but spelled differently—formed a team called "The Four Cristie's."

Individual bowling tournaments gave Cristie opportunities to compete with her age group as well as older children. After winning trophy after trophy, her mom and I began discussing future opportunities for college scholarships in bowling. As it became apparent bowling wasn't one of the more popular sports in Division 1 schools, we began to investigate other sports.

Cristie tried gymnastics and ballet, but she hated both. She was chubby and found it difficult to jump high enough to get over some of the equipment. She disliked ballet, since she had to wear a "stupid" tutu. Honestly, she did look quite out of place in it.

During my teenage years and in college, I enjoyed playing golf. As an adult, I stopped playing after I hurt my back in a car accident. Years later my back felt better, and I decided to play golf again. We joined the Kendale Lakes Golf and Country Club, a local public golf course. The membership included all greens fees for golf, use of the common areas including the pool, and a nominal charge for a golf cart. This soon became our family hangout.

In 1982, I started a second career as a teacher with the Miami-Dade Public Schools in Miami, Florida. Cristie's mom worked long hours in an attorney's office, so every day I picked up

Cristie after school and took her to the golf course, where I practiced and played nine or eighteen holes of golf. Cristie, who was eight, enjoyed riding in the golf cart as I played on the course for practice. When I was ready to putt, Cristie ran onto the green to hold the flag. She loved to run through the sand bunkers, which she thought was like being at the beach. Another favorite past time was throwing range balls at the fish in the lakes around the course, which she called "golf fishing."

Cristie was always around when I practiced. She was nine years old when she expressed an interest in hitting golf balls. I took an old seven iron, cut down to fit her height and began to teach her how to hold the club and swing. Soon Cristie wanted to learn to hit the ball far. No longer satisfied just hitting balls on the driving range with one club, Cristie wanted her own real set of clubs. I told her that before we would buy her clubs, she would have to practice to develop a good swing. We began practicing and I knelt down to tee up ball after ball on the driving range mat for her to hit. At first she found it difficult, but within a few weeks, she was able to make contact and hit the ball thirty to fifty yards.

Although Cristie was left-handed, I only could only demonstrate how to swing the club as I did, so I taught her how to swing right-handed. This became an advantage since her stronger left hand gave more power in her swing. At first Cristie hardly hit any balls, but as she practiced each day, she began to make better, more consistent contact with the balls. She began to hit balls in the air instead of on the ground. Balls began to fly thirty yards or more down range. This was the beginning of Cristie's love affair with golf.

Each day Cristie waited eagerly to be picked up from school to hit balls on the driving range. When she climbed in the car after school, her first words were, "Dad, we're going to the golf course to hit balls, right?" Soon I stopped my own practice to concentrate on helping Cristie improve her swing and make better contact with the ball. Initially, she only wanted to hit balls further and further, and she didn't care if balls went straight, right, or left, as long as the balls went far.

Cristie knew that I had other clubs in my bag, and she wanted to try to use these different irons and woods. She wanted clubs just like mine. Her enthusiasm for golf grew rapidly. *Whoosh!* Cristie learned how to swing the club faster and faster, and soon the balls were sailing down the range.

The distance markers on the driving range, which identified yardage distances, became her targets. To make practicing more enjoyable, I invented a game for her. If she could hit the distance markers at fifty yards, one hundred yards and one hundred fifty yards, I rewarded her with a treat on the way home. Each time she hit a distance marker, she would try harder to hit it again. The more times she hit the target, the bigger the treat after practice. Cristie was learning how to aim at a target and adjust her swing to compensate for the distance without even realizing what she was learning. As she became obsessed with this practice game, I soon was buying treats every day, usually a big, greasy burger, fries and shake, not the best choice due to the amount of fat and calories.

When Cristie was nine years old, I bought her a starter set of golf clubs. Now she and I were spending longer hours at the driving range. To teach her the use for each club, I demonstrated how to hit with each club. After hearing what each club was intended for and the type of shots the club was capable of making, Cristie loved the challenge of trying each of the clubs and imitating what I was able to do. Soon she was making the same shots using the different golf clubs.

When club members walked past while she was practicing, some would laugh and yell comments like, "Hey, Mike! What are you trying to do, make her into a Pro?" They didn't know that it was Cristie who was in control. She wanted to hit bucket after bucket. She was keeping me at the driving range, because she loved what she was doing, and it was fun. Soon I realized that I had taught Cristie just about everything I knew about the golf swing, and she needed a professional teacher and formal lessons.

CHAPTER TWO

The First Professional Teacher

    Tom Gibson, an apprentice pro at our country club and a very good golfer, became Cristie's new swing teacher. As her coach, I attended her lessons to be aware of what to look for as she practiced. Tom's teaching style and personality fit well with Cristie's, because he explained how to swing the club in a clear, uncomplicated way. He understood the components of the golf swing and made it easy for Cristie to follow. Because his teaching style had developed from working with other more experienced teachers, Tom was a good choice as a teacher for Cristie at this point.

    First, Tom changed how Cristie gripped the club. Although this was uncomfortable for a short time, Cristie quickly incorporated this new grip into her swing. Many players who change their grip struggle for months, but Cristie began gripping the club Tom's way as though she had done it from the beginning. Cristie had the ability to make changes in her swing quickly and with ease.

    Soon she began hitting golf balls towards the targets on the driving range. As her ability improved, she would look at me and exclaim, "Dad, look how far that one went!" Cristie wasn't concerned with direction or ball flight at this point, only how far she could hit the ball. She continued to make progress each day, because she insisted on hitting bucket after bucket of golf balls until she was wringing wet from sweat. This paid off as she began to consistently hit more good shots.

For the first six months, Cristie took lessons from Tom once a week, and she exceeded my expectations. Due to her rapid improvement, Tom increased his lesson schedule to twice and soon three times a week. In between lessons Cristie practiced, practiced, and practiced hitting golf balls for hours on end. Standing behind her or on the side, I watched every swing to spot her swing flaws, which had been corrected, and remind her of the position that Tom had taught for her swing.

After several months of observing Tom's lessons, I was able to spot when Cristie wasn't swinging correctly. I became like a video camera that spoke. When I pointed out a flaw in her swing, she would quickly correct it. As we spent endless hours at the golf club, I began to understand the mechanics of the golf swing from listening to all of Tom's lessons and observing Cristie practice.

To increase my own knowledge, I read many books and magazines about golf, studied videos of famous teachers, watched televised golf tournaments and paid particular attention to the announcers dissecting the player's swings. When Cristie was not practicing golf, she was usually doing homework or watching TV and was not interested in watching golf on television or listening to the analysis. Consequently, it became my mission to study the golf swing and learn as much as I could about the game, including *The Rules of Golf*. Watching the pros on television provided opportunities to observe rulings made during play. The rule book and the supplemental book, *Decisions on the Rules of Golf,* included not only the basic rules but also explanations for the interpretation of a particular rule. Understanding the rules is vital to the player, because a rule violation can result in having to add penalty strokes to the score or possibly being disqualified from the event. The rule book became my bible.

After eight months of lessons, Tom and I decided Cristie was ready to go on the course to play the golf holes, putting into action what she had been taught. Thinking this would be just like practicing on the driving range, Cristie was in for a shock! She didn't realize that playing golf on the course was totally different because the player only gets one shot, not a bucket of balls, to get it right. On the range, if the first shot wasn't good, the golfer can just dip into the bucket take another ball and hit it again and again until satisfied with the shot.

Initially, the golf course seemed like an easy place to play. With wide areas to drive the ball, the greens look very big, but Cristie quickly learned how difficult it was to hit the golf ball in the right place when she had only one ball and one shot. Standing on the teeing area, it looked easy, but there were hidden dangers. A stray shot could land behind, in or near a tree, behind or on top of a rock or roots from a tree, or even near or in a lake or stream. Additionally, the course was littered with different kinds of bunkers with sand of different depths and textures.

Cristie found out that her shots were not always perfect. Learning how to hit the next shot and recover from the strange places, where her ball rested, was not as easy as she thought. Cristie never got frustrated or mad if her shot landed in a difficult spot because she loved the challenge of learning how to make the recovery shot. Most golfers can hit the ball when it lies perfectly on a plush fairway, but the player who can make these unusual types of shots stands a good chance of scoring a low number on a hole in a tournament.

Between lessons, Cristie and I took a cart and a bucket of balls to the Jade Course in the late afternoon when no one was playing. I dropped balls in different places: behind trees or large rocks and even in-between the roots of trees. Cristie had to learn which club to use and how to recover from these types of places on the course. Over the next year, we practiced like this, and thousands of balls were thrown all over the course for her to hit to the green. She was learning how to scramble out of trouble, get the ball to the green to save par and at worst, make a bogey.

Now we began working in the sand bunkers, as I placed balls in the sand, burying them into the edges of the bunker, and sometime buried balls completely. Cristie had to learn to hit all different types of bunker shots, both long and short, into a green that ran uphill as well as greens that ran away from the player. After I buried balls in the worst possible places in the bunker, I demonstrated how to hit the shot. Then it was her turn to try to get the ball on the green. Cristie thought this was fun, especially when the sand she hit flew up in the air and into my face, covering me as if I had been buried in the beach. Every day she would practice hundreds of these types of shots. A ball lying in the sand for a professional golfer is an easy shot, but for an amateur player, especially a kid, it was very difficult.

A Father's Story

CHAPTER THREE
First Competition

Tom Gibson, Cristie's first swing teacher, told me about a junior competition sponsored by the Ryder Truck Company in Miami called the Doral/Ryder Pitch, Putt and Drive. Junior golfers would compete in age group categories by hitting three drives, three thirty-yard chips, and three thirty-foot putts. Points were given in each category and totaled to determine the winner and runners-up in each age group. Any child under age eighteen could enter by filling out a simple form. No entry fee was required because the event was sponsored by the Doral/Ryder Truck Company for the benefit of local area children.

If Cristie won her age group, she could advance to the semifinals a few weeks later. The finals were held at the Doral Country Club in Miami on the last day of the men's PGA Doral/Ryder Tournament. When the tournament players were all finished with the first tee, it would be used for the Pitch, Putt and Drive competition. What an exciting setting for kids, since thousands of people would be at the tournament; and perhaps hundreds would watch the kids. Pressure, Pressure, Pressure!

When this competition was described, Cristie became very excited and wanted to begin practicing to win. All she could talk about was, "I want to win this event, and I can win this event." Practicing every day for hours, she really didn't understand what was going to happen, but winning was her goal, whatever she had to do.

For the next six weeks, Cristie and I went to the golf course every day where she practiced with her driver, nine iron, and putter—the only clubs she would need. This competition, based upon distance and accuracy, awarded points for the longest drive, the closest thirty-yard chip to a target, and a thirty-foot putt closest to the hole. Cristie began hitting two, three, and even four buckets of practice balls every day.

Chip…putt…drive…chip…putt…drive. Hit the ball far, but hitting it straight was even harder. Hitting the ball straight is the most difficult skill to develop. It takes years of practice for a player to feel comfortable that the ball would go in the right direction. A few weeks into this practice routine, Cristie began driving the ball over one-hundred eighty yards, but not always straight.

Because she was hitting the ball so far for her age, people at the course started watching her practice. Many club players who couldn't hit the ball very far were amazed that a ten-year-old girl could do this. Soon people gathered behind Cristie, watching in amazement. We could hear comments like, "Wow! Did you see how far that one went?" or "It's amazing how this little kid can hit the ball so far. How come we can't do it?"

Cristie loved having people watch and admire her accomplishment. A real ham, she made cute remarks, knowing full well that her spectators were listening. This was fun. The bigger the crowd, the more she would show off. Hearing these compliments was much more enjoyable than the negative comments uttered just months ago. Club members began to see and understand her determination. One time she hit the ball well over 200 yards. As I watched the ball fly over the two-hundred-yard marker, I yelled to her, "Way to go, Boomer," and that name stuck with her for many years.

Six weeks went by quickly preparing for the biggest event in a young life. Cristie was driven and talked about winning as if it were the only thing that mattered. The competition was held at the Briar Bay Golf Club in Miami. While I wasn't sure how this competition was going to work, it was important that her mom and I would be there to watch Cristie compete for the first time. Hoping for the best, we had a feeling that she was going to come through like a champ.

When Cristie, her mom, and I arrived at the country club, hundreds of other parents were already there for the same reason: to watch their kid win. Boys and girls of all ages, from five to seventeen, would compete in age group categories. The winners and runner-ups in each age group would advance to the next stage, the Semi-Finals.

Cristie's mom and I were probably more anxious than Cristie, who was so focused with her eyes looking over the competition, getting a feel for what she was about to do. The youngest kids went first; and as we waited for her group to be called, she practiced, practiced, and practiced swinging her clubs. Finally, it was her turn. The driving competition was first. Cristie stepped up to the tee, put a ball down on a tee, then went through her pre-shot routine. To me, she looked like a Pro who had been doing this all her life.

Other parents gathered around to watch the competition, hoping, just as we did, that their kid would win. Cristie's first drive wasn't too good, long enough, but not inside the target area. The next drive was hit hard and long and went straight down the target area, where it was measured at 199 yards. Other parents and spectators were amazed seeing a ten-year-old hit a drive that most adults could not do. Spectators began yelling and cheering for Cristie, because they couldn't believe what they had just seen.

In my excitement I yelled, "We're on the way to the LPGA!" While I drew several strange looks from the crowd, I had just seen my daughter hit a drive farther and straighter than she ever done before. It even surprised me! Cristie got a lot of points for that drive and went on to come in first in the chipping and putting. She won her age group. Now the next goal was to win the semi-finals in two weeks at the Biltmore Golf Club.

A Father's Story

CHAPTER FOUR

Gearing Up for Competition

Once again Kendale Lakes Golf Club would be our daily place to practice for the semi-finals. With practice in high gear, two to three hours a day, I made it clear to Cristie that competition would be tougher in the semi-finals because winners and runners-up from the different quarter-final locations would be in this next competition and only two from each age group would advance to the finals.

The semi-finals arrived, and for a child this anticipation might be like what a pro would feel preparing for a PGA Masters Tournament. Cristie was ready and played well but came in second. This was good enough to go to the finals, and she was eager for redemption. With two weeks before the finals, the anxiety level began to rise. This could be her first rite of passage. Could she do it under the pressure? During the weeks before the finals, Cristie was so focused that she and I had little time to think about anything else except practicing. To keep her from developing anxiety, I spoke very little about the finals.

After weeks of preparation, my whole family arrived at the Doral for the tournament: my parents, Morris and Ethel Kerr; sister Laura; Cristie; my wife Linda and I. Because we were four hours early, we had plenty of time to eat and watch the Pros tee off. Tension and anxiety began to rise in everyone, except Cristie. In an unusually quiet mood, Cristie was visualizing her game plan. My parents didn't understand much about golf or this competition, but seeing the crowd at the Doral prompted many questions about what was going to happen. Cristie's grandparents were very excited and overwhelmed by what was going on around them.

Practicing was not possible until all of the Pros were off the driving range. At most, the kids would have only about a half hour to warm up before the competition began. As Cristie was warming up, I saw the tension in her eyes and she became snippy. For the first time I saw nervousness poking through her seemingly calm exterior. Wondering if this would be her undoing, I attempted to keep her calm as she kept insisting that she was all right and ready.

When the last group of Pros finished playing the first hole, kids and parents swarmed to the first tee area for the start of the competition. To my amazement, hundreds of people were lining the fairway to get a good view. These spectators, who had come to watch the Pros, had heard about this tournament and wanted to watch the kids compete.

As Cristie stepped up to the tee, we all held our breath waiting for her to draw back her driver. *Boom!* She hit the ball in the target area but only 176 yards, which gave her 17.6 points. Her chipping and putting were fabulous, and after the last putt dropped, we waited for the final totals. Cristie lost by three-tenths of a point. With a drive just two or three yards longer, she would have won. As far as her family was concerned, Cristie was a winner. After two stages of competition, she reached the finals and almost won. Everyone was proud of what she had accomplished except Cristie, who wore her feelings on her face,

A Father's Story

no matter how much encouragement came her way.

This loss hurt, and took her weeks to get over the disappointment of being so close to winning. This was the first of many losses to come. To truly appreciate winning, a player needs to experience the feelings and frustrations of losing. After about two weeks, Cristie put this loss behind her and was ready to get back to taking lessons and continuing to improve her swing.

Weeks later, Cristie stated that Doral would be the only time she would lose because she was going to work even harder and predicted a win the next year. Golf is a strange and frustrating game. Players lose lot more often than they win, but learning how to handle a loss will turn the experience from negative to positive for future events. Learning to handle a loss mentally is a difficult even for a Pro but especially for a very young, inexperienced amateur. When things go wrong in a tournament, the player can bring negative thoughts to the next tournament. By learning from their mistakes, players benefit from the experience so that in the next similar situation, they react and play better than before.

Cristie began asking about playing in more tournaments, because the desire to compete helped her to forget the loss at Doral. With a skilled golfer as a daughter who was focused on playing and winning other tournaments, my task was to find more competitions appropriate for her age and skill level. We wanted to start with events which were close enough to our home, as well as affordable, so that she could gain experience without becoming discouraged with competition that was too stiff for her ability. Tom suggested that Cristie play in the local Junior Golf Association tournaments in Miami. This would give her the opportunity to gain experience playing against kids her own age and ability.

CHAPTER FIVE

Using New Technology

Early in March, Tom Gibson started videotaping Cristie's swing during her lessons. Watching herself in slow motion, Cristie could see which parts of her swing were not in the proper position and needed to be adjusted. With each lesson, Cristie understood more and more about her swing. Cristie had an ability to see a problem and correct it within a short period of time, usually after hitting one or two buckets of practice balls.

Tom thought that the Dade Amateur Golf Association (DAGA), which ran tournaments for the local kids in Miami, was a good place to start. When I mentioned this to Cristie, all she wanted to know was, "When can I play in these tournaments?" DAGA's Spring Break tournament was held in April. As Cristie's tournament fever began to rise, her desire to compete and win could be seen in her preparation.

Now Cristie was practicing with all the clubs in her golf bag. Seeing her practice longer and harder with a renewed enthusiasm, I felt that tournaments gave Cristie a new level of energy and excitement. Her internal drive to consciously prepare for competition was so strong that even after hitting two to three hundred range balls, she would often say, "Just one more bucket, Daddy!"

We spent every afternoon and early evening at the golf course. After observing her lessons with Tom, I would watch her swing and make corrections as she practiced. Because the short game was my forte, I was able to teach her to hit all kinds of shots from many different places.

The short game in golf refers to the shots players make from various positions close to or near the green. Because players can make a variety of shots from the same distance, the type of shot required depends on the location of the ball and the position of the flag on the green, as well as any obstacle the player has to avoid so that the ball comes to rest as close to the hole as possible. At times a player has to hit a shot that has a very high trajectory so the ball will land softly and not roll. Other times the player may hit a low shot that will bounce onto the green and roll to the hole. Although there are special clubs that make the ball fly high or low, a player may also use other clubs by adjusting the ball position or position of the club face during the swing as well as the length or arc of the swing to make the ball fly as desired.

The ability to make these shots with different kinds of clubs requires a tremendous amount of practice and an understanding of what will affect the shot. Wind, depth and type of the grass are factors that can affect ball flight. Cristie's ability to learn and become proficient in these different shots quickly made her more proficient than me. How exciting it was to watch my daughter show such great talent for golf!

Her main problem was that during tournaments Cristie's scores were still over one hundred. While she was able to make the shots in practice, she found it quite different in a tournament when she had to do it on the first try. No matter how frustrated, her reaction was to get better and improve her swing.

Determined that her scores would get lower with each round of golf, Cristie constantly insisted that she was going to practice even harder to win the mini-tournaments. Having her goal as getting the beautiful trophies for first, second and third place finishers, Cristie wanted most of all, the biggest trophy given to the winner, which she hoped to bring home soon!

Before her dream of winning could come true, Cristie needed to learn more about parts of the game, specifically how winning players manage themselves during a competitive round of golf, which is called Course Management. A great player understands what club to hit off each tee, to put the ball on the fairway or close to it so that the next shot to the green is clear of obstacles. It is much easier to hit greens when the player can hit the ball over, under or through openings between trees or behind boulders or in the deep grass. This is a mental skill that must be developed.

Teaching a player which club to use, what part of the green to land on, as well as what parts of the course to keep the ball away from helps a player shoot lower scores. Many golf fans have watched well-known players lose the lead on the fourth and final day of a tournament due to choosing the wrong club for their tee shots on the last few holes. Even the best pros on the tour do not always make the right decisions. Under pressure, when pros are not able to do what was best to win, the mental game gets to them.

Incorporating the mental game into the physical game made Cristie's development more complicated. Determined to do whatever it took to accomplish her goal, Cristie had to make choices. Golf was consuming all of her free time, but she was willing to give up a lot. She would practice instead of spending time with her friends, going to school parties and events, shopping in the mall and just hanging out. These were decisions she made. Most girls her age would find this difficult, but

Cristie's love for competitive golf overshadowed everything. She practiced in the rain to become familiar with what she could expect to do under conditions that were less than perfect. The better she got, the more Cristie practiced, and we would often stay at the golf course until late in the evening practicing under the lights.

CHAPTER SIX

Swing Changes and Learning the Rules

Tom Gibson began to change Cristie's grip to promote a better, more consistent swing that would result in better shots. Whenever a player makes a change, no matter how small, it takes a while to adapt to the new grip. Most adults take months to adjust to these changes, but Cristie was able to make adjustments very quickly. There was no magic in being able to do this, just hard work and hitting hundreds of practice balls. At the end of many days, Cristie was wringing wet from sweat, her hands hurt, and she was physically and mentally exhausted.

Tom would give her one lesson each week at the beginning, while I stood on the side or behind her, correcting each of the swings she made. Suggestions like, "Keep more weight on your right side, or start the down swing with your legs, not your upper body," were understood, and Cristie could make small corrections with ease. As she started to improve, she took lessons twice and sometimes three times a week. Each lesson reviewed what had been taught before as well as introducing something new. Tom was amazed at how Cristie was able to incorporate everything he was teaching so quickly. Her dedication to practicing increased as the days went by.

A Father's Story

The best score in golf is the lowest score in contrast to other sports where high scores win. A round of golf has eighteen holes, and each hole has a score assigned called Par. Each time a player hits the ball, it counts as a stroke; and at the end of the round, the player with the fewest strokes wins. Most courses are made up of four Par 3's, four Par 5's, and ten Par 4's. Par is the number of strokes a player should make on a particular hole, and when all eighteen holes are added up, the score should equal 72, which is playing the round in Par. The object of golf is to score Par or better. Scores higher than Par are not good, but scores below Par are great. Names are given to each score above and below Par: one under Par, Birdie; two under, Eagle; one over, Bogey; two over, Double Bogey; and so on. Occasionally, a player will hit the ball into the hole on the first shot. This usually is done on a Par 3 and is called a Double Eagle or "hole in one." Players who score lower than Par are usually professionals who have been playing golf for many years and are playing to win money as well as trophies. Amateur golfers, who play for trophies, usually do not score close to Par.

Learning to understand and follow *The Rules of Golf* was part of the preparation for tournaments. Knowing the rules would give Cristie the opportunity to understand when she might have to take a penalty as well as how to take advantage of a rule which would give her a better position for the next shot. Generally, players are governed strictly by the rules of golf during tournaments organized or sponsored by a golf organization whether they are playing for prizes or money. Important tournaments have rules officials, who assist the players in understanding the rules, infractions and penalties, if any.

The United States Golf Association (USGA) publishes *The Rules of Golf*, a complete listing of all rules, and a supplemental book that explains the rules in more detail, including special conditions pertaining to that rule. With limited knowledge of the rules of golf, Cristie needed to read and understand the rule book, which she would carry in her golf bag. While there were so many rules, she needed to learn the most common ones and be able to reference the others in the rules book. This part of her golf education would be ongoing, as she also continued to improve hitting the ball in the right place and getting it into the hole.

Golf courses have grass, and sometimes lakes, streams, and ponds. While the fairway grass is short, the grass off the fairway is called the "rough," and can be four or five inches long, which makes it very difficult to hit the ball far or straight enough because the grass acts as a barrier between the club and the ball. When a ball lands behind a tree or some other obstacle which makes it impossible to hit the ball, the rules allow a player to take relief and move the ball into a better position, but this results in a penalty stroke being added to the score.

Because golf does not have a "do-over shot," Cristie needed to learn how to play from these unusual places by practicing those shots on the course. Learning how to get the ball back into the fairway requires the skill to hit unusual shots and the ability to analyze the situation and evaluate different strategies before hitting the ball. Teaching Cristie how to handle these situations became the toughest part of her golf education. Learning to hit the ball from tall grass, behind trees, from sand bunkers and hundreds of difficult places took understanding, patience and practice. Thinking about shot options and how to best advance the ball required hitting thousands of practice shots from the worst possible places and understanding the percentages in making the shot.

This process involved more than just a few lessons. No longer was Cristie just working hard to build a repetitive golf swing.

A Father's Story

Now I was helping her develop "The Mental Game." Great ball strikers with weak minds don't perform well under pressure, and this process would last for years. While this was the most frustrating part of the game to learn, Cristie wanted more than anything else to become a professional golfer on the LPGA and play golf rest of her life. At that time she wasn't interested money or celebrity. She wanted to become one of the best and win a whole bunch of tournaments!

CHAPTER SEVEN

First Victory

In May 1989 at age twelve, Cristie had her first victory. After playing for two years in DAGA's junior golf tournament at the Mel Reese Golf Course in Miami, Cristie was finally rewarded for all the hard work when she won a tournament in the third flight. Boys and girls of equal playing ability composed each flight, and the best players in the Dade Amateur Golf Association competed in first flight. Age meant nothing, ability ruled.

One year and five months from the first lesson to the first win. In the next tournament, Cristie came in second and was moved up to the Second Flight. Now she would play against older boys and girls with better golfing ability. During the next tournament held at the Doral Park Silver Golf Course, Cristie shot the best round of golf in tournament play with an 86, which won the event in the second flight.

Breaking 90 and shooting 86 was an extremely difficult, and this accomplishment gave her a tremendous amount of confidence. Determined to shoot even lower, Cristie played in eight more DAGA tournaments during the summer of 1989. With seven wins and one second place, Cristie began to fill our home with trophies, displayed on the coffee table, the living room hutch and even in the bathroom. Her second attempt at the Doral/Ryder Pitch, Putt, and Drive Tournament was another pivotal point when she won. After winning by a large margin, she considered it her first major because the year before she lost by three-tenths of a point.

Having outgrown playing in local tournaments, Cristie was ready to play against older and better competition. Because she was unbeatable locally, she needed experience in nationally ranked tournaments. I knew this step up in competition would frustrate her. She would lose many tournaments. Losing is the only way to learn by mistakes and turn losing into winning. She needed to compete against the best that the nation and world could offer. To play in these prestigious tournaments, she had to be invited based on her resume of tournament accomplishments. The national tournament committees only wanted the best junior golfers in the world in their field of players. Since these tournaments did not have age group categories, the field of players would include girls from all over the world, many three to six years older than Cristie with national tournament experience.

Other than winning local tournaments, Cristie's golf resume was not yet impressive. Golf resumes list how a player performed in tournaments, and players with national experience were in a better position to be invited to the more important tournaments. Being accepted in a nationally ranked tournament was not easy, especially if a player had never played in one before. Somehow, I had to find a way to get her invited to play in one of these events, hoping that she would finish in the top twenty and begin to establish a resume that would identify her ability in playing against tougher, more seasoned players.

While Tom was an excellent swing teacher, he couldn't spend enough time with Cristie on the golf course working on the other parts of her game so that became my job. From this point forward, the focus of my life became helping Cristie during her practice and also on the course to develop the other parts of the game that Tom was not able to teach due to his time constraints. I also felt that Cristie's next teacher needed to be someone with experience teaching professionals, who could guide me in helping Cristie reach her goals. From this point forward, golf for me was on the back burner. Cristie's future was in my hands, and I was determined that she would succeed.

To help Cristie continue to improve her game, I became a student of golf. I watched top pros teach on television, watched videos on all phases of golf instruction and read just about anything I could get my hands on. Whenever I was in the presence of golf professionals, I initiated a conversation about golf and the mechanics of the swing. I was quite surprised to find out how similar professionals were in some areas but how completely different they were in their approaches to teaching the swing and the mechanics of the swing. All agreed upon one particular idea: what the player's arms, legs, body and club would look like at the time the club head made impact with the ball.

After studying many of the top professional players on the tour, I saw a variety of different looking swings, but when their swings were slowed down on video, the position at impact was exactly the same. Cristie and I watched some of these videos, and as I stopped the action to show her their positions in the swing, she began to develop a mental picture of what she was being taught to do. This made it easier for her to understand what she did well and what needed to be changed.

CHAPTER EIGHT
Going National

Manasquan, New Jersey was the site of the 42nd United States Golf Association Junior Girls Championship in August 1990. This tournament had a different format than any other which Cristie had played. The field of one-hundred fifty-six girls would play two rounds of golf; and at the end of the second day, only players with the best sixty-four scores would advance to the next stage of the tournament, "Match Play."

Match play is a single elimination format where the player with the best score (*first seed*) over the two days plays the player with the sixty-fourth score (*last seed*); the second seed plays the sixty-third and so on. Only the winners of each match advance. The match play segment starts with sixty-four players. The thirty-two winners advance, then the sixteen winners advance, then eight, also known as the quarterfinals, and then four play in the semi finals. The final round crowns a winner. In the end, the winner of the tournament would have played two practice rounds, two qualifying rounds, and six rounds of match play. This was not only a test of golfing ability but of physical stamina as well.

Tom and I discussed this tournament and the benefits for Cristie. We agreed that if Cristie could get invited to play in this tournament, she would benefit from the experience. Although we thought she probably wouldn't win, she had a good chance of making it to the top sixty-four players after the first two days. Playing in a tournament of this magnitude was above her head at this point, but she would gain immeasurable experience. We mailed the application and waited for the selection committee to respond, because getting an invitation to this event was tough, since the selection committee chose only the best junior girl players in the world under age eighteen. In amateur golf for juniors, this tournament was considered to be the toughest and best in the world, the "Major" of girls' junior golf.

Meanwhile, Cristie was making good progress with her game. Her swing was beginning to repeat, or look the same, each time. She could drive the ball longer than most girls three to five years older. In fact, she was longer off the tee than most women amateurs and some pros as well.

After what seemed like an eternity, the letter finally arrived from the USGA. Cristie was accepted! We were going to Manasquan, New Jersey. Her acceptance was a great surprise, considering the talent available from all over the world. Cristie had an impressive resume of wins and second place finishes in our local tournaments, but nothing compared most of the other players.

The trip to New Jersey would include the cost of travel, the hotel, food and other expenses for Cristie, her mother and me. Rather than spend money on three airfares, we decided to drive, so we bought a new van. Our family was so excited about the trip that we lost our sense of financial management, which became an important part of travel to tournaments in future years.

Traveling around the country playing amateur golf costs as much as a professional. The big difference is that amateurs win trophies and the pros get cash and a trophy. When Cristie first became involved in national tournaments, her mom and I were able to scrape together enough cash using credit card advances and loans from family members and friends. As the travel became more frequent, we became stressed to finance these trips. Many of our credit cards were maxed out, and we faced tremendous financial pressure. When Cristie's mom inherited land in North Carolina, she sold this land to pay for the golf expenses. We were determined to do whatever was necessary to give Cristie the opportunity to become a professional golfer. Fortunately, some family members provided some assistance.

The trip to Manasquan, New Jersey took over twenty-four hours. We drove most of the trip through severe thunderstorms. When it was still raining fifty miles from the destination, we wondered if we had made a long trip only to find that the tournament had been cancelled due to bad weather. Within ten miles of Manasquan, the sky turned blue, the rain stopped, and out came the sun as we arrived at our hotel, exhausted by the long drive. Tournament golf was here.

Wonderful experiences for Cristie filled the next few days. As the youngest player ever to be invited to play, the USGA made her feel welcome and comfortable by arranging a caddie, who was the son of one of the members and the current club champion. Parents were not allowed to caddie for their kids, a rule which the USGA adopted to avoid arguments between the parents, rules officials, other parent caddies or the kids themselves. Knowing the course, Cristie's caddie helped her with yardages, club selection and reading the greens for putting, because he knew the best place to position the ball for the easiest putt.

Unlike the flat greens in Miami, slopes and hills made it very difficult to tell which way the ball would roll. Sometimes a player could not aim directly at the hole and would have to aim two to four feet right or left of the hole to allow for the ball to curve to the hole. This was the toughest part of the game for Cristie, who had never played on greens like these. With the grass cut short, the ball rolled very quickly, making it even more difficult to judge just how hard to hit the putt. Hit too hard and the putt might come back that was longer that the one before.

During the two practice rounds on Monday and Tuesday, Cristie's caddie kept telling me how impressed he was with her ability. He thought she could win this tournament, but I don't think he was watching the other girls too closely, because the competitors were all terrific golfers with experience on courses in tournament condition like this. Only making suggestions to Cristie about her game, I hoped she would concentrate on what she was doing, not on what the competition was used to or capable of doing. While I kept assuring Cristie that gaining the experience from this tournament was quite an accomplishment in itself, she could only think of winning. With hills, blind shots and tall pine trees lining both sides of the fairway, this was an awesome test of golf for Cristie as well as the best of these girls.

A Father's Story

CHAPTER NINE
Tournaments and the Media

Cristie played better than I expected, but she had difficulty on the fast greens. While she wasn't able to get the feel of the putting speed and made few pars, her play brought raves from many parents, coaches, and members of the golf selection committee, who felt she had performed wonderfully given her age, difficult conditions, pressure and competition. While she needed more experience to be competitive, everyone hoped Cristie would advance to match play.

As the qualifying tournament was coming to a close, Cristie and other players who were close to the sixty-fourth score, or "The Cut," crowded around the scoreboard. Keeping a watchful eye on the players on the course, the girls hoped to make it into match play if some players made mistakes and did not score well. At the end of the day, sixty-four players' names were listed on the board, and a big red paper cut-out of a scissor marked the name of the last player. Tears, sobs and regrets from players who missed the cut filled the air, Cristie included. Words cannot explain how disappointed Cristie felt, but the tears in her eyes told the story. She was exhausted, sad, disappointed and unusually quiet after five hard days of practicing and playing.

The trip home seemed to take forever. The mental stress had taken a toll on the entire family, but we talked to Cristie about the great experiences she just had and how what she had learned from this tournament would help her in years to come. Having competed at the highest level of junior golf, Cristie had an opportunity that only a handful of female golfers experience. We were convinced that bringing Cristie to this tournament was the right decision. While experiencing losing, she gained a tremendous experience on the beginning of her long journey to become one of the best. Now I needed to develop a game plan to help Cristie continue to increase her skills and prepare for the future.

The one thing that I did not prepare her for was the amount of press coverage that she received. The print and television media were all over her for the first few days. While loving every minute of the interviews and spotlight, Cristie was not prepared to answer the questions from the media. This was another skill that Cristie would have to learn. Giving interviews and answering questions posed by experienced reporters is not easy. Practice and coaching in interview skills were needed to come across in a polite, positive manner. Because Cristie needed professional help in this area, I had to find someone from the media in the Miami area to teach her the art of being in the spotlight.

As a confident player, Cristie was so focused at times on the course it appeared she didn't see anyone or anything else. If this were perceived as being aloof, she could have become a target for negative press comments. Being strong-willed and having difficulty opening up to the media, Cristie had to learn to be cheerful and available for interviews. Like many players, Cristie had to learn to hide her emotions, especially after a bad day on the course. Players must develop self-control and concentration to be warm and friendly after a round of golf they would like to forget.

Cristie's focus on the course was so intense, at times she appeared unapproachable to spectators. Becoming "fan friendly" is a learned skill which doesn't happen overnight. Understanding the media and what and how they write, can make or break opportunities for future endorsements. Media can be a player's best friend or worst enemy, because what and how they write sells magazines and papers. Because spectators may form opinions quickly, Cristie's golf ability might be only a small part of public impression of her personality and as a golfer. Improving her persona toward the media and spectators before, during, and after golf tournaments was necessary to insure positive public opinion.

Cristie Kerr

CHAPTER TEN
Dade Amateur Golf Association (DAGA) and Charlie DeLucca

During the summer vacation from school at ten years old, Cristie started playing in the Dade Amateur Golf Association's tournaments, where I met Charlie DeLucca. This organization provided kids of all ages and backgrounds with the opportunity to learn golf and play in tournaments during the summer break from school. The young golfers played in "flights" grouped by age. Occasionally, younger players competed against older, more experienced players if their golf skills were beyond those of their own age. The younger kids played a nine hole weekly tournament, and the older, more advanced golfers played eighteen holes.

Dade Amateur Golf Association (DAGA), organization provided opportunities for the youth of Miami-Dade and surrounding counties to play golf. In 1977, a national organization called The First Tee was organized, and Charlie became the Executive Director of the First Tee Miami-Dade Amateur Golf. The opportunities provided by Charlie DeLucca's organization gave many children, especially those economically disadvantaged, an opportunity to participate in golf. Since 1997, The First Tee has spread to most of the states in the USA.

Beginning his career in 1962 as Head Professional for the Miami Lakes Country Club, Charlie DeLucca served in many prestigious golf organization committees and advisory boards. In 1999, he received the Special Olympian Humanitarian award and was also responsible for passage of legislation for the golf license plate. For over forty years, Charlie DeLucca has been recognized as a great teacher and role model for pros and amateurs in the game of golf.

Shortly after Tom Gibson moved out of town, I approached Charlie DeLucca during one of DAGA's weekly tournaments and asked him to teach Cristie. Soon Cristie and I made a daily trip to his driving range at Mel Reese Golf Course, near the Miami Airport. Charlie began helping Cristie and soon their relationship would become very close. Being around Charlie DeLucca and his staff of highly competent teachers, including his son, "Charlie Boy" and Charlie Piefer, was very important. Cristie took to Charlie's teaching style immediately and absorbed everything he told her. Charlie became like her second dad. When Charlie wasn't around, the others would always help Cristie.

More than just a place to hit golf balls, Charlie DeLucca's driving range was a local gathering spot, where kids and adults would spend afternoons and evenings taking lessons, practicing, and socializing. Charlie would move up and down the range, providing help as encouragement or a simple adjustment to a swing; no one was ignored. After advancing rapidly, Cristie began to playing against older players, mostly boys, and she was beating them each week. Charlie DeLucca was a dynamic influence in Cristie's life.

Cristie Kerr

CHAPTER ELEVEN

A Turning Point

In December, Cristie was looking forward to two Florida golf tournaments: The Doral-Ryder Junior and the Junior Orange Bowl. The preceding three months were filled with preparation, especially on her short game, her weakest area. Many players can hit the ball far with a driver, three-wood or an iron, but when the ball is three to twenty yards off of the green, these players take too many strokes before the ball gets in the hole.

A player may make many different shots from these positions, but using the same club with a different type of swing can generate totally different trajectories and spin on the ball. Each shot can result in the ball either coming to rest quietly on the green or racing across the green and ending up far away from the hole. These are called finesse shots, which can make the difference between winners and losers. The weeks of preparation were exhausting as Cristie hit over one thousand range balls each week: long, short, shorter...chip, pitch, chip, pitch, high shots curving right then curving left and then low shots doing the same and, of course, putt, putt, putt and more putting. To dominate, Cristie knew she needed an outstanding short game, and her goal was to develop the ability and confidence to step up and hit the ball in the intended distance and direction.

In past years, Cristie never won The Doral-Ryder Junior Classic. This tournament, which attracted over five-hundred players of all ages from all over the world, was one of the biggest junior golf tournaments with most of the best international players. Cristie's first experience in the tournament was on the nine-hole Green Course, where she came in fourth. After having to withdraw the following year due to a knee injury, Cristie was determined this year would be better.

On the first day of competition, Cristie shot 87. During the next round, she missed too many greens with her approach shots. She had to rely on her putting, which also let her down. Over the next two days, I witnessed a turning point in her game as she began to hit shots that landed on the greens and make par putts. The hard work was beginning to pay off, as she shot 78 and 76 in the second and third round, but her score (87) on the first day put her in a disappointing third in her age group.

Another prestigious junior golf tournament, played during the school winter break is the Junior Orange Bowl Golf Tournament in Miami. This tournament was part of the Orange Bowl events prior to the college Orange Bowl Football Game. With the help of Charlie DeLucca, who was the head of DAGA and also on the Junior Orange Bowl Committee, Cristie obtained an invitation to play in this tournament. The field of players was particularly strong with many players from foreign countries as well as girls from the USA who played on the national junior circuit.

While playing well in this tournament, the defining moment was on the 18th hole. Starting with a good drive in the fairway, her second shot ended up in the tall grass eight feet from the green. With four-inch grass, Cristie could not see her ball. Using a sixty-degree wedge, Cristie hit into the area where the ball lay. The ball jumped out of the grass with a high arc and landed a few feet from the hole. This type of shot is very difficult even by professionals, and Cristie was only twelve years old.

The crowd went wild! Her fourth place finish gave her a tremendous amount of confidence as well as establishing her as the young player to watch in the future. Ordinarily, a fourth place finish goes unnoticed, but Cristie had played against the best junior players in the world and finished higher than most. She received plenty of media coverage in the local paper as well as the local television stations that covered her story. She was the hometown girl who had just accomplished what they did not think anyone her age could do.

A few months after the Orange Bowl tournament, Cristie received a letter from Jim McLean, who operated the Jim McLean Golf School at the Doral Country Club Resort in Miami, Florida. His facility, located at the back of the driving range, was well known world-wide. Visitors and local residents flocked to his school to take lessons. With a reputation as one of the best teachers, his schedule was very full during the year. Jim also conducted golf clinics for kids to improve their golf skills. Many aspiring young teaching golf pros wanted to work for Jim to be able to add the name Jim McLean to their resumes and to try to attain Jim McLean's certification as "Master Teacher."

The letter to Cristie was very complementary, because Jim saw her potential for professional golf. When Cristie used his practice facility, Jim helped her improve her swing. Cristie was excited to work with someone the PGA pros came to see for help. Over the next few years, Cristie practiced and played almost exclusively at Doral. The high-tech video equipment helped Jim and Cristie to immediately see her swing. This was a great diagnostic tool.

CHAPTER TWELVE
The Junior Golf Tour

Because only a few tournaments are scheduled from January through March, most junior golfers work on their swings and try to improve their skills for the upcoming tournament season. Cristie worked very hard preparing to play in American Junior Golf Association (AJGA) tournaments. As the recognized leading junior golf organization, the AJGA was host to over twenty-five top quality tournaments each year. A very selective resume process was used, and no one outside of the organization knew the selection criteria. Each player submitted an application with a tournament resume, hoping to be accepted.

The goal of the American Junior Golf Association, like the United States Golf Association, is to assemble the strongest field of players at each event. The emphasis on players in the fifteen- to seventeen-year-old age group provided opportunities for junior and senior high school students to showcase their talents for the college coaches who attend these events. Players' performance in tournaments could make or break their chances for college scholarships. Most players were older than Cristie, and very few younger players were invited to play.

As I filled out applications for Cristie, I was confident that her fourth place finish in the Junior Orange Bowl would give her access to some tournaments. After applying to three, Cristie was accepted to two and was called at the last minute to fill an opening in a third tournament in Arizona. Most players were juniors or seniors in high school, which left little room for a thirteen-year-old to play, but on occasion someone withdrew due to injury or illness and a replacement was needed. A player called to play at the last minute must drop everything to get the first flight out, but this opportunity would improve her resume for future events.

The AJGA tournaments in Texas, Hilton Head, and Arizona were far from successful for Cristie. Her drives kept her in the desert, putting her in a position to chip out, often resulting in bogeys or worse. Having difficulty getting the feel for the greens covered with a very short grass called "bent grass," her putts were very fast. With undulations all over the place and greens which were not flat, Cristie had trouble judging the direction of the putt and which way the ball would break. Experience is needed to play these types of courses. Growing up in Florida, Cristie was used to playing on courses which were basically flat with a different type of grass. With no way to simulate these other course conditions, Cristie had to learn to play under these new conditions.

The presence of the top players in junior golf may also have been intimidating on this difficult course with greens fast enough for the pros. This could be frustrating for a young golfer who may want to make excuses or explain why it was hard to play well. As a parent and coach, I had to learn not to expect too much too soon. Frustrated parents may offer advice such as, "If you go out and do your best and play badly, that's one thing, but don't make excuses to avoid accepting your responsibility!"

These words don't help a distraught young player who is not playing well. Because I wanted Cristie to succeed so much, I sometimes forgot that she needed time to grow up and mature. Her golf ability sometimes exceeded her emotional ability to handle frustrating situations.

Fortunately, Charlie DeLucca gave me good advice that all good players go through a period of adjustment when their physical ability exceeds their mental and emotional development. Eventually, one would catch up with the other. Because he did not explain how long this might take, I had difficulty communicating with Cristie, and at times she became defensive and resistant to listening to my advice.

When Charlie DeLucca said these things, Cristie reacted in a more positive way. Observing how Charlie was less critical and much more complimentary, I decided to do things his way, because Charlie was getting the results that I couldn't. As an outsider, Charlie could set aside emotion and talked to Cristie in a soothing, calm manner, and she reacted to his style much better than to mine.

Charlie DeLucca taught me how to develop a better, non-emotional method of communicating with Cristie. I learned how to manage my emotions and talk about the things she did well instead of criticizing what she did wrong. Charlie was right, because golf is about ninety-percent mental and positive reinforcement would always be accepted. I hoped to continue this in the future, and I needed to learn to be less direct and more subtle. This was a hard part of the role of both parent and coach.

CHAPTER THIRTEEN

Playing Against Adults

With the school year coming to an end, Charlie DeLucca's role with Cristie became more of a mentor than a teacher. After asking him to become her next full time teacher, I was thrilled when he accepted. In addition to his magnetic personality, everyone raved about his teaching ability and devotion to helping young talent develop. Having worked with several men and women who were touring pros, Charlie DeLucca's personality and teaching style could help Cristie because he could critique her game without evoking a negative reaction, which helped her develop a better public persona.

Charlie's calming influence on Cristie gave her an added measure of self-confidence. As she listened to him, Cristie began to understand what people expected of her in addition to playing great golf. Charlie DeLucca saw her talent and took a keen interest in her as a person, not just a player. Cristie was not the only young player that benefited from Charlie's influence. His love for golf motivated him to work with young players without any expectation of a future return other than the satisfaction of helping. Charlie was regarded locally as an outstanding golf professional that put the interest of others ahead of his own.

The Women's Amateur Public Links Championship (WAPLC) was a national women's tournament. To play in this event, Cristie had to qualify in a one-day tournament at Mel Reese Golf Course in Miami and finish first or second. The WAPLC, The Women's Amateur, and the Women's Western Tournaments were the big three national events. Because all three required qualifying to get in, the field of players included many of the strongest women amateurs in the world. Cristie played exceptionally well in the qualifier, not only advancing to the tournament but also walking away with low medalist honors with a score of 76.

The University of Virginia's Birdwood Golf Course held a surprise for our next tournament. This hilly course had trees everywhere, with blind shots to greens hidden by the hills. Because Cristie was only thirteen years old playing in an adult tournament, I was allowed to be her caddie. In addition to carrying her golf bag, I helped her calculate the correct distance to hit the ball to the green for the best position to putt for a birdie. While she was in control of her game, as her caddie I helped her make club selections for different shots.

When Cristie and I, as caddie and player, were working well together, we discussed what would affect the shot, both what might happen when the ball was in the air as well as when it landed on the green. Wind, ground terrain, where and how the green slopes all had to be considered before Cristie could make a decision where to aim and how far to hit the ball.

Most caddies are young adults, because the job involves physical endurance, carrying a golf bag five or more miles, up and down hills. When I caddied for Cristie, I was over fifty. Golf bags can weigh between twenty to forty pounds depending on the weather, and when the weather was bad, I carried extra towels and rain gear, which added more weight. At the end of the day, I often used ice bags to ease the pain on some part of my body. Younger caddies made remarks to me and laughed, all in good fun, but this was a tough job, which I loved. Being a caddie gave me the opportunity to help Cristie, and I was in the middle of the action with the best view.

As many competitors, as well as spectators, noticed this unknown girl playing so well, I heard complimentary talk about her play. Some wondered if they were watching the next superstar coming out because Cristie not only was the youngest player in the history of the tournament to qualify but also the youngest to make the two-day cut.

The press was swarming around Cristie for interviews and pictures. Cristie handled herself well due to the help from a golf writer with the *Miami Herald*, Dave Shinen, who had taught Cristie interview techniques and how to answer questions asked by the media. The combination of help from Charlie DeLucca and Dave Shinen paid big dividends because now Cristie was coming across with maturity and confidence and did not appear arrogant. The press reacted well to her approach.

While she did not win, Cristie gained national experience and increased confidence in playing against adults, many who had golf scholarships in college. This tournament was an important learning experience for Cristie and me. When playing in a national event, especially against adult women, some act surprised when a younger golfer plays better than they do. Not wanting to lose, especially to a teenager, the players watch everything that happens on the course. The experienced players are aware that the novice's knowledge of the rules is limited. When they saw a younger player breach a rule, an official was immediately called to determine if a penalty was appropriate.

This lesson was learned quickly. Cristie was playing in the first round of qualifying for match play with two women who were playing poorly. After hitting a ball which landed on the left side of the fairway in the short rough, Cristie's swing would be hindered by a tree behind her with moss hanging from the branches. The rules of golf state that a player cannot make anything fall or break from the tree behind the golfer while taking practice swings, since that would be considered "improving the intended path of your swing" and would result in a penalty.

Stepping back three feet from her ball, Cristie took some practice swings, and moss fell down. The players who saw this called an official, who asked Cristie to demonstrate what happened. As her caddie, I had seen the entire incident better than the other players who were on the other side of the fairway, where they did not have a clear view of the practice swings. Although Cristie's practice swing was far enough away from the ball, she was given a penalty because some moss did fall.

The rules official probably believed what the older players described was correct. When I tried to give my opinion to the official, I was told "Mr. Kerr, we only talk to the player, not the caddie!" Feeling insulted and angry, I told the official this ruling was unfair and incorrect, but I quickly learned that officials look at caddies as just another piece of equipment. Officials only want to hear from the players. Cristie, intimidated by this situation, was afraid to be forceful enough to make her point understood.

Cristie played Naomi Korashima from Japan in the first round of match play. Korashima had finished the qualifying rounds in second place and was one of the players that everyone expected to win the tournament. To the astonishment of all, Cristie was beating her one up after eleven holes, but Korashima's experience prevailed and Cristie lost on the sixteenth hole after making three consecutive bogeys.

Korashima capitalized on Cristie's mistakes. My chest was bursting with pride! We went home with Cristie engraving another notch in the golf history books as the youngest player to qualify and make the cut at Women's Amateur Public Links Championship.

A Father's Story

CHAPTER FOURTEEN

The Summer Tour

During June, July, and August, most nationally ranked junior golf tournaments are played. A premier event hosted by the Professional Golf Association (PGA) called the PGA Junior attracted over fifteen-hundred kids from over forty state qualifying tournaments, all trying to earn a spot in this tournament. Held at the PGA National Course in West Palm Beach in August, Cristie won the South Florida PGA Sectional with scores of 74 and 75, beating the entire field by fourteen strokes. Cristie was going to the finals and was continuing to establish herself as one of the nation's top players. No more the up-and-comer. She had arrived!

The summer golf tour was an eight-week, non-stop marathon. Because I did not teach during the summer, I traveled with Cristie. While her mother did not travel with us because she worked in a legal office, Linda was involved in planning and handling the logistics of our travel. During the school year, I had to take many personal days and days without pay to travel with Cristie to all her tournaments.

A third place finish at The Naples Beach International, followed by tournaments in Oklahoma, Missouri, Chicago, and

Kansas, brought us back home in early August. Cristie played well but didn't win any tournaments. This summer we decided to economize on traveling by trying something different. After comparing the cost of flying, renting cars and staying in hotels to renting a motor home and driving to the tournaments over the summer, I decided to rent a twenty-two foot motor home where the first tournament started in Edmond, Oklahoma. From there I drove to the other tournaments, finding this motor home very small even for two people. Using the bathroom, cooking, and showering were very uncomfortable.

In addition, no one ever told me about the difficulty finding places to park overnight or where to flush out the small holding tank. Finding RV parks was so difficult that I had to find places to park at night while we slept. One morning we awoke to find that I had parked in a cemetery. Many nights we were chased out of parking lots in shopping centers and had to find roads away from the main road just to park. Cooking was so difficult that we ended up eating fast food and saving no money on food. In fact, we spent more than our budget. Occasionally, we were allowed to park in the golf course parking lots. With limited availability of electrical outlets, we ran out of propane gas. What a mess!

An experienced motor home traveler, who planned in advance and had a vehicle at least thirty-five feet long, might enjoy this method of travel. The rental company failed to inform me about items not included which needed to be purchased. I also had not considered potential breakdowns and the time and cost to get things fixed. I drove three thousand, six hundred miles that summer while Cristie slept in the bed during much of the trip. I was wiped out. This six-week trip cost more than flying, renting cars, eating out and staying in good motels.

On the way to Chicago, we stopped in Springfield, Missouri for the United States Golf Association (USGA) Women's

Amateur Qualifier, but Cristie failed to qualify. In Chicago, she played in the USGA's Junior Girl's Championship, finishing the stroke play portion at 150 and seeded in the sixth position. One year ago, she shot two rounds of 88 at Manasquan, New Jersey and missed the cut. This year she shot 80, 70 and finished sixth with the low round of the second day. Although she played well in the stroke play portion, she didn't play well in match play and lost after the second round.

While Cristie did not win during the summer of 1990, she continued to gain more experience. These tournaments were filled with outstanding players who had more experience playing in tournament conditions with deep roughs and fast greens. While seasoned golfers had an advantage, I was confident that Cristie would emerge as one of the top players, but in the meantime the growing pains were tough. In the coming months, Cristie did lose often, but then she began to dominate the tournaments as no one in junior golf had done before. What she and I needed was patience. We needed to replace frustration by concentrating on all of the positive things that happened to get ready for the next tournament.

CHAPTER FIFTEEN
Moving Up In Class

In December 1991, Cristie competed in the sixteen-to-eighteen age group at the Doral/Publix (*formerly Doral/Ryder*) Tournament. Charlie DeLucca and I felt this age group competition was closer to the national tournaments, and I couldn't identify a stronger player than Cristie. While this was a very large tournament, with over five hundred kids from ages eight to seventeen, the field included many girls who had competed in United States Golf Association or American Junior Golf Association events during the year.

This tournament is always held during the school holiday break in December. While many of the better female golfers who had been playing all year long wanted to be home with family at this time of year, plenty of girls from other countries came to Miami for this tournament and a vacation with their family. Because many of these girls played internationally, we were sure that some would be strong players, but Cristie was playing against the course as well as the other golfers.

Cristie began with a strong round of 75, placing her in second position at the end of the first day. On the second day, she continued with a strong front nine, scoring one over (37). The next nine holes were disastrous, and she shot 47! Trying not to make mistakes, she had problems with club selection, distance control and direction. Sometimes trying not to make mistakes leads to self-destruction.

I held my breath on every swing during that nine holes and wondered when she would get her game back. Finally, Cristie got it back together and shot 38 on the back nine. We went back to the clubhouse to watch the scoreboard and found that Cristie was in a four way tie for second. The leader, Erica Hayshed of Peru, had an overwhelming lead of seven shots.

The next day was filled with anticipation. Could Cristie hold on and come from behind to win or finish second or at least in the top five? On the last day, the top sixteen girls played the Blue Monster course, the longest and most challenging of the five courses at Doral, with plenty of sand bunkers, trees, tall grass in the rough and water.

At the end of the fourteenth hole, Cristie and Ann Tinning from Denmark were tied. Everyone was watching Cristie and Ann in a real battle for second. First place was just about guaranteed for Erika Hiashida, who was ahead by a comfortable seven strokes. The battle for second came down to the last hole. Many great professional golf matches have been won and lost on the Blue Monster's 18th hole.

Cristie hit first with a long drive into the right rough, safe from the water on the left. Her ball nestled down in the deep rough of St. Augustine grass, which is tough to hit from and has been the cause of many errant second shots to the green. Ann's tee shot was also in the rough. She hit first and her ball stopped seventeen feet from the flag. Now the pressure was on Cristie. Would she choke?

After selecting her club and going through her routine, the ball took off straight for the flag, took two bounces, bit and spun back just six feet from the cup! This was the best shot that Cristie had made in a tournament. Cristie proved to herself that she had what it takes to become a great champion, the ability to make the shot when the pressure was on. Ann missed her putt. Cristie made hers and came in second.

A Father's Story

CHAPTER SIXTEEN
The Doherty Championship

The Doherty Tournament drew the best in women's amateur golf. After playing an eighteen-hole qualifier, Cristie finished like a true champ as the eleventh seed in the bottom quarter of the sixty-four player draw. Not wanting to become a "Cristie Kerr casualty" began to bring out the best in Cristie's opponents. With a reputation spreading throughout the golf world as the next great player, even though Cristie was only fourteen, she brought fear into the hearts of her competition. While Cristie didn't win every time she played, she definitely was one of the players to beat in any tournament.

In the Doherty Championship in January 1992, Cristie's first opponent played extremely well but lost to Cristie one up after twenty holes. Cristie could have beaten her sooner, but as it happens in match play, her opponent dropped three long chips and three long putts to stay alive in the match and force it to go two extra holes. Cristie's next opponent, Moira Dunn, was the best player on the Florida International University team. Later that year Moira won the Women's Western, considered one of the two top women's tournaments in amateur golf. Moira made some great chips and long putts. Cristie came back to even when she reached the eighteenth hole only to lose on the first playoff hole. Both Cristie and Moira had twelve-foot putts. Cristie missed; Moira didn't. While this was a great match, Cristie took this loss very hard. She felt that the tournament rested on this match, since all the ranked players had been beaten in their matches prior to Cristie's match.

Time heals wounds, and in golf, time allows players to forget losses and move on to the next tournament. The Junior Golf season began with the first tournament, the MCI Heritage Junior Classic held at Hilton Head, South Carolina. Cristie finished a disappointing sixth behind a weak field of players. Over the two days, she drove the ball with precision, hitting fourteen fairways, but was unable to hit more than three greens on the first day. Tee shots averaging 220 yards were followed by shots to the green from 90 to 120 yards, only to fall consistently short of the green.

With some swing problems, Cristie was not accelerating through the shot, causing the ball flight to go right or left of her intended target. Players are not robots. While thousands of practice ball fly week after week, other factors can contribute to a swing fault. Physiological problems such as fatigue and stress can change a woman's rhythm, affecting her swing. On the second day, more great drives and better second shots resulted in scoring a respectful 76.

On the long drive home, Cristie and I had plenty of time to review her performance at the tournament, particularly her short game. Over and over we looked for answers for the cause of the swing problems but we were stumped. I kept wondering, "Was she just playing safe and trying not to make mistakes?" We could not identify anything that would cause her to hit the ball with the correct club only to have it land short of the green, especially since the wind had not been a factor. The weather had been great, the conditions were perfect, and the course played as benign as any course could.

By the time we arrived in Miami, I thought the problem might be her equipment. Her swing looked too perfect for such poor results. The more I thought about this, the more I became convinced this was the problem. Cristie had grown taller and gained some weight. Just two weeks prior to this tournament, she hit a new driver and three metal woods (*wood clubs were now obsolete*) and decided these were better than her older clubs. The new Yamaha driver and Taylor-Made three metal wood helped tremendously. The overall increase in club weight helped Cristie control her tempo, but she was still playing with her old irons. These irons appeared to be the reason for the problems she was having on the course. Her game now required a custom fit set of irons.

The golf clubs sold in stores are sets made for the average player. Custom clubs are made to fit, taking into consideration the player's height, swing speed and strength. While the club head is the same, the golf shafts come in a wide range of materials. Some shafts are flexible, and some are stiff. Some are made of steel, and some are made out of graphite. Each shaft has a spot on the shaft called the "flex point" that determines where the shaft will bend during the swing.

Some players have each shaft matched by frequency vibration so all shafts feel about the same. Once the correct shaft is selected, the player is custom fitted for "loft and lie," which is how the club head sits on the ground when the player addresses the ball and the angle of the club head to an imaginary line that is perpendicular to the ground. Lofts and lies control the distance and trajectory of the ball. Even the type and size of the golf grip is well thought out. After the player hits these custom fit clubs on the driving range, small adjustments are made from the player's comments about the feel of the club, the launch angle and trajectory of the ball.

This process is usually reserved for a professional who uses clubs as part of an endorsement to promote the club manufacturer's promotional advertising. We didn't have this luxury, but I was able to borrow several new sets of clubs for Cristie to try. After hitting everything available, she liked the feel of the Tommy Armour 845's irons, and we both noticed an immediate improvement in her distance control, accuracy and ball flight. Her old tempo returned.

Apparently, Cristie's old clubs were too light, causing her to swing too fast. These 845's were heavier and apparently better suited for her at this time. She looked forward to the next tournament to prove that her swing was solid and that her problems had been due to old equipment. Her new irons produced an immediate improvement on the course. While Cristie regained the confidence she had lost at the tournament, one more adjustment was needed. These clubs were manufactured with standard lies, which is the angle the bottom of the club sits on the ground when holding the club to hit the ball. The lie has to be adjusted to the player's height and length of arms. If the lie is not correct, the ball will not go straight. From the moment the lies were adjusted, Cristie's shots to the green started to land all around the flag. She couldn't wait for the first American Junior Golf Association tournament of the year at the Woodlands in Houston, Texas on March 17th, 1992.

CHAPTER SEVENTEEN
A Tough Spring Break

During the spring break of April 1992, Cristie and I went to visit Tom Gibson in North Carolina. After moving from Miami to North Carolina the prior year, Tom had become the head professional, general manager and equity partner at a course he helped find for investors he met in Miami. This was a wonderful opportunity for Cristie to work with Tom again on a golf course that was closer to the conditions of the Woodlands Golf Course in Texas, the site of her next tournament. It was a long twelve-hour to drive to North Carolina. When we arrived, the wind was howling at thirty mph, and the temperature was in the forties. Not exactly what we expected, but golf isn't always played under perfect conditions.

Cristie was hitting the ball quite well, but Tom's golf course was in poor condition. The investors were planning improvements that were scheduled to be started later that spring. Had I known the condition of the course, I might have made other arrangements for Cristie to practice on a course similar to the Woodlands. The long winter and unusually cold weather for March had taken a toll on the grass. Fairways with sparse grass made it difficult to hit the ball, so we decided to travel south to find better playing conditions for Cristie.

We drove to Orlando to play the Magnolia Course at Disney World. Cristie's game was as sharp as ever, and it felt good to return to the warm weather. We didn't even have time to visit the area attractions. All of her thoughts were only on one thing: winning The Woodlands Tournament the following week.

The Woodlands Country Club and Resort, which hosts the first American Junior Golf Association tournament of the year, is a beautiful venue for the season's first event. Our arrival on Thursday, March 16, 1992 gave Cristie time to play a practice round the next day. Cristie began to warm up by hitting several buckets of balls, and then she moved over to the practice bunker. After putting for over an hour, she returned to hit just a few more balls to loosen up before her practice round. Watching her hit with confidence, I had a good feeling that she could win this tournament.

Suddenly, as she hit the last ball, Cristie screamed in pain. Everything appeared to go into slow motion. I saw her begin to fall as her left knee collapsed. As I rushed forward to catch Cristie, her screams got louder and pierced the air. Everyone around stopped what they were doing and looked to see what was happening. This was serious, and everyone knew it!

Within two hours I was able to get Cristie to a local orthopedic doctor recommended by one of the tournament officials. After a brief examination and x-rays, I was told that Cristie would need a MRI to confirm his diagnosis: a torn or severed anterior cruciate ligament and tear of the meniscus cartilage. He put her in a full Velcro cast from her ankle to her hip. If the doctor's diagnosis was correct, surgery would be required, which I felt would be better if we were at home. An operation this serious would keep Cristie out of golf for at least a year, possibly longer, depending on the severity of the injury. It could mean the end of golf completely. Her mother booked first class airline tickets to get us home as fast as possible on an emergency basis. We needed to fly first class, because Cristie was wearing a full flexible cast on her leg and needed extra space to keep her leg elevated to reduce the swelling. She was in severe pain!

On the flight home, the pilot had to fly around severe thunderstorms, which caused us to arrive late. The following day at the Doctors Hospital in Coral Gables, we met with Dr. Keith Hechtman, recommended as one of the best orthopedic surgeons in the area. The exam and MRI confirmed our worst fear: her ACL was severed. Torn meniscus cartilage also needed to be repaired. A complete reconstruction of her knee was needed, and at least nine months of physical therapy rehabilitation would be required. Golf would be out of the picture for a year or more. Cristie was in so much pain that all she could think about was feeling better, and the idea of an entire year out of golf was not an issue. The only thing on her mother's mind and mine was getting her healthy and free of pain.

After the initial shock of the severity of her injury, Cristie wanted to get better and play golf again. Before even starting rehabilitation, Cristie could only talk about golf, golf, golf! Injuries are part of all sports, but this was an injury caused in part by Cristie fooling around in the front of her school while waiting to be picked up. While chasing a boy, she caught her sneaker in a drain, and the twisting caused the rip in her knee. Had I known about this before, precautions could have been taken to let it heal. When young people become trained athletes, avoiding some of the childish games and horseplay is appropriate, but it is hard to convince a teenager.

Cristie's desire to practice and compete made it worse. Cristie did not tell either her mom or me about the initial injury at school because she believed that she had just strained her knee and it would get better on its own. First and foremost we wanted Cristie to get better, but we all knew that this could have been her best year with successful tournaments. While I was worried about her future as an athlete and a golfer, I was also determined not to let an injury, which could heal, destroy her career because of worried parents. Now everyone would have to wait.

The surgery was performed at Doctors Hospital at 6 A.M., Friday, March 24, 1992. It seemed like forever before Cristie was moved into intensive care; and after three hours of recovery, she was taken to a private room, groggy, but she still managed a smile. Cristie was happy the surgery was over, but now months of physical therapy lay ahead. When the morphine wore off, Cristie was in terrible pain. The pain medicine didn't relieve the pain, and the doctors were reluctant to give her too much at one time.

On the Monday following her surgery, Cristie began therapy at the Health South Rehabilitation Center. Cristie missed several weeks of school but was able to do schoolwork at home. She returned to school, using crutches for many weeks. Every day I took her to therapy, five days a week for the next five months. Cristie also had to exercise at home between visits. With her focus on her rehabilitation for the first five months after surgery, playing golf was not on her mind. Only as she began to feel better did she begin to get the itch to play tournament golf again.

Determined to get better, Cristie would do her exercises with more repetitions than required and push herself more than any other patient at rehab with the same injury. Her goal was to rehabilitate this knee as quickly as possible and get back to golf. After all, The Rolex Tournament of Champions in Tucson, Arizona was in November, and she was determined to play.

A Father's Story

CHAPTER EIGHTEEN
The Road Back To Golf

After three months, Cristie's therapy had been reduced to three times a week by June 1992. While she felt strong enough to want to hit soft, short pitch shots at the driving range, a doctor's approval was needed to allow her to try. Dr. Hechtman said that as long as Cristie did not put too much weight on her left knee, and did not allow it to torque or twist, she could begin to practice again. Being able just to put a club in her hand and make short swings gave Cristie encouragement that golf was in her near future. She could not have done this without the unbelievable amount of time spent in therapy and her willingness to endure the long hours of exercise and cold icing after each session.

To help Cristie return to her playing form before the injury, she needed a professional teacher who had worked with other golfers with similar injuries. While still far from complete recovery, she was progressing in the right direction. When I called Tom Gibson to recommend a teacher, he thought that Bob Toski would be able to help her get back into playing shape, since Bob had worked with many other pros with injuries. I contacted Bob Toski and set up a lesson. Well-respected as a teacher, Bob Toski was a great player and everything he said was precise and clear, but he and Cristie didn't develop a rapport. After several more lessons, Cristie and I decided to look for a different teacher.

Cristie's light practice was months ahead of Dr. Hechtman's timetable. Because her endurance was low, she could only hit one bucket of practice balls a day. Unable to put much weight on her left side, her knee couldn't handle the twisting motion just yet. As weeks passed, she began to feel more and more confident. Moving her weight from the right side to her left side while swinging was difficult for her physically and mentally, because she was afraid of reinjuring her knee.

At the end of the fifth month, Cristie's knee was much stronger than anyone expected. With therapy workouts becoming longer with many more repetitions and strength exercises, the data from Biodex Tester machine showed a thirty-percent deficiency in her quad muscles, but her hamstring muscles were very strong. I kept asking the therapist for an opinion of when Cristie would be able to swing the club with full force. While I was anxious for approval for Cristie to begin going all out, Dr. Hechtman was conservative, saying, "We'll see next month." The doctor felt Cristie should wait a full year, but I understood Cristie's burning desire to get back into tournament play.

Because her knee no longer hurt when she moved or bent down, Cristie became more aggressive with her golf swing during practice. I watched every swing for any sign of a reason to stop, but she looked strong and felt good. When asked about Cristie's concern for reinjuring her knee, the therapists assured me this was typical of most patients in the recovery process and that her knee was probably stronger than before the injury. Cristie began to feel confident that her knee would hold up to the strain of the golf swing. Because Cristie wasn't finishing completely on her left side, she began to hit the ball with a sweeping hook. This problem, which took months of dedicated practice to fix, turned out to be more of a mental issue than physical disability.

Cristie went back to work with Charlie DeLucca at Mel Reese. I felt confident that he could work out her swing problems, because she trusted him and what he said. I was able to schedule time when Charlie could devote his complete attention to her. We were very fortunate because Charlie DeLucca's schedule was full of clients wanting lessons, but he always set time aside for Cristie.

CHAPTER NINETEEN

Back to Tournament Play

With the Dade Amateur Golf Association beginning the summer golf season, Cristie felt it had been a long time since she had the thrill of competition and wanted to play. While this was not competition at the level she had experienced, after nine months of not playing, Cristie was anxious to get back in the game! We began at Miami Shores Country Club, where Cristie played in the last group since she could not walk or play fast enough to keep up with the other players. In the final group, she would not hold up any other groups or slow down the pace of play. If she were not able to finish playing, I could put her in a cart and drive her back to the clubhouse.

Cristie was smiling again. With the worst behind her, she could look forward to getting back to what she loved more than anything else, tournament golf at the national level. Cristie was three months ahead of schedule. Because I did not expect her to be able to play so soon after the surgery, I had not applied to any tournaments during July and August.

I called the PGA to ask if Cristie could get into the field for the PGA Junior at the end of August, since the qualifying rounds were rescheduled due to rain. Although she was exempt from the first qualifier due to last year's sectional win, she was not allowed to play because the application had not been completed and filed by the deadline. While she was disappointed, I was determined to get her into a tournament soon.

After hearing about a junior tournament in Tampa, I called, and Cristie was accepted. Soon we were on our way to East Lake Woodlands Country Club near Tampa, Florida for a three-day tournament. The practice round and three days of walking put quite a strain on her knee. This became her first true test of golf and endurance since her injury, and it was the beginning of Cristie's return to tournament golf. Four days later, scores of 73, 82, and a last day's score of four under Par (69), Cristie won the girl's division by 39 strokes! We didn't care that the top players in the country were missing, because it was a win. This win was against the golf course, and more important, a win Cristie would never forget after her injury in Houston, Texas almost ended her golf career.

Cristie was looking forward to playing in the Ray Floyd Turnberry AJGA event in late August in Miami. Unfortunately, we had missed the entry deadline, but the tournament gives an exemption to the local golf association. The Dade Amateur Golf Association gave it to Cristie, who was eager to play. We checked into the Turnberry Resort to give Cristie four days to practice on the course. While this course wasn't exceptionally long for the girls, it had several tricky holes.

Cristie was paired with Kellie Booth and Wendy Patterson, two of the stronger nationally ranked players. Finishing third behind Wendy by one stroke, Cristie had an opportunity to win, but four double bogeys over three rounds proved to be too much to overcome. Since she was still hanging back on her right side and hooking the ball, this event identified swing problems to be addressed in future lessons and practice.

Cristie Kerr

CHAPTER TWENTY

Golf After the Hurricane

In August of 1992, Hurricane Andrew hit Miami leaving everything in a mess! Homes were destroyed and schools were closed for two weeks. Nearly every business in the south end of the county had been destroyed, which meant that every practice facility in Miami-Dade County was closed. Over the next four months, I looked for places for Cristie to practice. The only facilities open were in Broward County. A sixty-mile round trip became a daily routine for the next seven months until the facilities in Dade County would reopen.

With his driving range closed for six months, Charlie DeLucca wasn't available to help Cristie due to the many problems he had solve to get his course open for play. This was a tiring time! As a teacher, I heard many stories of displaced families struggling to rebuild their homes and their lives, but I knew if I did not continue to work with Cristie, even under these difficult circumstances, she might lose her opportunity to get back into competitive golf.

When one of the first golf courses to open was Kendale Lakes Golf Course, we were thrilled to have a driving range so close to our home. Still, Cristie needed a teacher because Charlie wasn't available. Meanwhile, I had been watching a young teaching professional at the Kendale Lakes Golf Course named Scott Jones, who had a grip on the golf swing and the mechanics involved. Scott agreed to work with Cristie, just two weeks before she would play in a lower level tournament in Marco Island, Florida sponsored by The Ping Jr. Tour. This lower level tour event gave her the opportunity to play under tournament conditions without the pressure of a national event. Within a few weeks, Scott had helped Cristie return to hitting the ball close to her skill level prior to the injury.

The Marco Island event was good for Cristie. She placed second behind Betty Chen, who was ranked fourth in the Junior Girl's Rolex Rankings by one stroke. Cristie had an opportunity to win; but on an easy Par 3, she hit the ball over the green, made a double bogey and finished as runner-up.

Hoping to win her next tournament, she continued to work with Scott Jones over the next two weeks. Following Cristie during the Marco Island event, Scott learned more about her game and identified what needed to be improved, especially her play out of the sand bunkers. Cristie accepted his advice without question.

At the next event in Dallas, Texas, Cristie won by beating Betty Chen by two strokes with scores of 76 and 79. The toughness of the Bear Creek Golf Course, the cold weather, and difficult playing conditions were more reasons to celebrate. The next two weeks were filled with anticipation for The AJGA Rolex Tournament of Champions on November 23, 1992 at the La Paloma Golf Course in Tucson, Arizona. Cristie was automatically entered into this tournament based upon her record with the AJGA.

CHAPTER TWENTY-ONE

*Making Friends and Gaining Recognition
in National Competition*

The Rolex Tournament in Tucson, Arizona brought Cristie back into playing in nationally ranked tournaments. Anxious to compete against the best junior players, Cristie wanted to try again to succeed under the pressure of national competitive golf.

During her practice round, Cristie played with several Korean players. Over the next few days, friendships were made that would last many years. Grace Park, who was thirteen years old, tall, and physically strong, was considered the next young star of junior golf. Soon Cristie and Grace became good friends.

Their friendship gave me the opportunity to get to know her dad. Although he spoke little English, we were able to understand each other by talking slowly and using our hands and facial expressions. Over the next few years, we spent a lot of time together when our daughters were playing in the tournaments. The Park family owned a beautiful home in Phoenix, where we enjoyed socializing and eating wonderful Korean food prepared by Grace's mom.

The two days of stroke play took place before the field was cut from forty players to the top sixteen. Cristie missed being

Medalist by one stroke, only to be beaten by Kellee Booth who lost in the first round of match play to Skylee Yamada. Cristie beat Kelley Keene, Heather Bowie, and Jaime Kazumi, who was young enough to play junior golf but already a freshman on the Duke University team. Cristie beat some of the best of players only to lose in the finals to Wendy Patterson.

Cristie was tired, lost her focus and got whipped, down seven holes with six to play. Runner-up in this tournament was an accomplishment which helped Cristie move up in the national rankings. *Golfweek Magazine's* national rankings are based on a point system awarded to the player's performance in tournaments according to many factors, including the strength of the field. This was a sixty-point tournament for Cristie; and just ten months after her surgery, Cristie had almost taken the crown jewel of American Junior Golf Association, "The Rolex Tournament of Champions."

With December and the Doral/Publix and Orange Bowl tournaments just around the corner, Cristie and I were confident she was ready for that first national win—perhaps even two, back to back. The Doral Golf Course was Cristie's favorite, and she was very familiar with the courses at Doral, having played there many times. While this year's tournament was loaded with strong players, Cristie won by shooting a tournament record for three days of 218.

The tournament ended with an awards ceremony, where trophies were awarded to kids of all ages. By the time of the awards were presented to the oldest winners, most parents had left to prepare for their trips home. At the closing ceremonies and awards for the oldest group, only Cristie's immediate family and a few tournament committee members remained. Everyone else was on their way home.

Although Cristie had accomplished a golfing milestone in this tournament, little fanfare was paid at the end. The next day, the local newspaper, *The Miami Herald,* published a comprehensive article with some great pictures of Cristie. She was a hometown hero.

The Junior Orange Bowl Tournament was held a few days later in Coral Gables, Florida at the Biltmore Golf Course. Cristie came in third due to poor putting. It became apparent that we needed to focus on putting, especially the three- to eight-foot putts. Making putts from these distances is crucial to winning. This was confirmed at the MCI Tournament in Hilton Head, South Carolina. After an opening round of 72, Cristie led the tournament then three-putted six greens on the last day and lost to Ann Pohira by one stroke on the 18th green. Ann played the best round of her life and sank a forty-foot putt. Cristie made bogey.

During the AJGA Woodlands Tournament in April 1993, Cristie kept hitting the ball into the fairway bunkers. Once in these deep, red clay bunkers, she had trouble getting to the greens on the second shot. On the first day, with great conditions for scoring, Cristie shot 80. On the last day, Cristie shot 76, which tied her for seventh and still seven strokes from the leader, Kellee Booth.

Improvement was needed with her course management, which caused Cristie to make mistakes in club selection and what type of shot to play. At times she played too aggressively when she should have been more conservative, and sometimes the opposite situation occurred. Because Cristie was not thinking on the course as well as she was able to hit the ball, this part of her game was holding her back from winning tournaments. Learning to visualize the greens with the slopes and hills and understand where to hit the ball on the best part of the green would give her a better chance of making birdies and pars. Even the best professionals find it difficult to score when they are in the wrong place on the green or just off the green, where recovery shots are needed to save par on the hole.

CHAPTER TWENTY-TWO

Entering High School 1993

Since age ten, when Cristie began practicing at the Kendale Lakes Golf Course, Daryl Baker had been watching her development. As the golf coach at Sunset High School, which Cristie would attend, Daryl saw her talent and wanted her to play on the high school golf team—the boy's team, that is. In 1993 this was still a radical idea, since the high school golf teams throughout the state of Florida were single sex golfers.

Daryl came from a golfing family and his two brothers were professional golfers. Gary Baker had played on the PGA Tour for a few years. All three Baker brothers were really good players. Having caddied for Gary, Daryl knew golf and was anxious to have Cristie on his team.

Sunset High School had enough boys for a team, but not many girls went out for golf. While Cristie was in middle school, I spoke with Daryl Baker about Cristie playing on the boy's team and the problems she would have as the only girl, if not the first girl, ever to play on any boy's team in the State of Florida. We could expect some resentment from the boys, since Cristie could probably beat most, if not all, of them. Coaches of teams from other schools might also be resentful.

We knew it was one thing for Cristie to play against girls and win; but when girls beat boys, younger or older, it could become an ego problem for the boys. Daryl was sure these problems could be overcome, because he had confidence that as Cristie's golfing ability became known, she wouldn't be considered just a girl playing on the boy's team; but hopefully, she would be perceived as the golfer to beat on the Sunset High School Golf Team.

When the golf season began, Cristie practiced with the boys every day. Additionally, she practiced individually with me, as she had for years. The high school golf matches were only nine holes, generally held after school. At times, the team traveled to more distant courses and had to take time away from classes.

From the very beginning, our family agreed that if Cristie were to play on the boy's team, and continue to play in tournaments on weekends and during the summers, she would have to maintain a good grade point average and do all the lessons and homework required by the teachers. Her education was as important as winning golf tournaments. Cristie would not be considered for a college scholarship to a good university if she did not demonstrate academic as well as physical ability.

An excellent student, Cristie approached school the way she approached golf. Striving to be an "A" student, she always completed her assignments on time. While some student athletes receive accommodations with teachers providing an alternate, easier assignment or extending a due date, this was not the case with Cristie, who never asked for any concessions and always did the required work on time. From the beginning of ninth grade, she maintained a straight "A" average.

When the golf season arrived, Daryl chose only five players to play the golf match. His decision was made after watching them play nine holes against each other the day before the tournament and using the best five scores to select the five players for the tournament against the other school. Generally, the lowest score on those nine holes determined the number one player, the second lowest score would be the number two player, and so on down to number five. Daryl also brought several additional players to the matches in case he had to replace a sick or injured player.

During the first few preliminary matches to determine the order of play, Cristie didn't play well so Daryl played her somewhere in the middle of the group. After a few weeks in which Cristie still was not performing well against the boys in these mini-tournaments, I took her aside with the coach and told her, "If you're not going to play your best, then quit the golf team, and concentrate on the national junior and women's amateur events. If you want to be on the boy's team, you have to go out and beat them, which is what you are capable of doing, if you want to gain their respect."

It seemed that Cristie wanted to feel welcomed by the boys on the team and may have thought that losing by a few strokes would gain their friendship as well as their respect. Quite the opposite occurred since the boys did not respect Cristie for any reason. When Cristie started to play to her ability, she started beating the boys by a large margin, not by just one or two strokes. Now they began to respect Cristie as the best player on the team, not a girl playing on a boy's team. She became "one of the boys."

Cristie made friends playing on the boy's golf team. Relationships based on athletic competition are very different from the typical teenage flirting and dating activities. While most male golfers are more powerful and can easily beat their female contemporaries, benefits develop from coeducational teams in sports which depend on individual skill. For example,

Alex Fernandez, her best friend and a good golfer, began to play better because of Cristie's presence on the course.

As soon as Cristie established herself as the number one player on the Miami Sunset High School boy's team, they began to win almost every match against other schools. Because Cristie was just about unbeatable by the other school's number one players, this frustrated the other coaches. As Cristie's skill increased, other golf coaches did not want Cristie playing on the boy's team. Some had just about resigned themselves to losing every time they played Sunset High School because of Cristie. Unknown to either Daryl or me, many coaches throughout Florida tried to have Cristie removed from the boy's team, claiming that she should be playing on the girl's team.

The State of Florida's Athletic Association had a clear position of girls playing on a boy's team: if there were three or less girl players on a team, then a girl may play on a boy's team. Four or more girls would constitute a girl's team, which would require Cristie to play on it. Fortunately for Cristie and the boy's team, most girls at Sunset didn't like golf, which was all right with us.

The experiences playing on the boy's team in high school were good for giving Cristie the opportunity to play against golfers who hit the ball farther than she did. This made Cristie think herself around the golf course and use all of her skills in pitching, chipping, and putting to beat them. This was good practice for Cristie for future tournaments against the nationally ranked girls in the country. The Sunset High School golf team did very well for the two years that Cristie played on the team. The Sunset golfers went to the State Championship, where they were very competitive even though they did not win.

Cristie played on the boy's golf team during her ninth, tenth and eleventh grades. In April 1993, the high school golf season had just a few tournaments left: the Dade County Youth Fair, the

Greater Miami Athletic Conference (GMAC), and the District and State High School Championships. The GMAC was held at her home golf course, Kendale Lakes Country Club. After having difficulty initially playing in a hard rain, Cristie improved and managed to tie for first then won in a three-hole playoff. Cristie had now won two of the three tournaments.

One week before the GMAC tournament, Mike Phillips, a *Miami Herald* sports writer, wrote a beautiful article on Cristie in which the headline read," KERR'S LONG DRIVES, FUTURE SHOULD GO A LONG WAY." He called her "Sunset High School's female phenom," and she was proving this in every tournament she played. In keeping with her new nickname, Cristie was honored by the *Miami Herald* as a co-player of the year.

A Father's Story

CHAPTER TWENTY-THREE

Burning the Candle at Both Ends

The district finals involved a series of events, which required Cristie and me to drive up and down the State of Florida, from Miami to Daytona and back, twice. Cristie was going to try to qualify for her first Ladies Professional Golf Association (LPGA) tournament, the Sprint Classic. Every Monday prior to a tournament, the LPGA allowed certain classes of professionals or amateurs to try to qualify for two spots in the tournament. The two players with the lowest scores after a one day 18-hole tournament qualify.

After a practice round on Sunday, Cristie ended up in a five-way tie. The four professional players and Cristie went into a playoff for the two spots. After all five hit their second shot to the green, Cristie and one other player were in the greenside sand bunker. Cristie hit second, and her ball came to rest just two feet from the hole. One player made a par, the other three made bogeys, but Cristie birdied the hole and qualified. The pros couldn't believe they had just lost to a teenager.

We headed back to Miami for the District tournament. By becoming the youngest amateur to qualify for a professional tournament, Cristie was on the verge of becoming a celebrity.

The *Miami Herald* ran a big article about what Cristie Kerr had accomplished, but this was just beginning. She now had to play in the district finals.

As soon as the district finals were finished, Cristie and I drove back to Daytona, where she played in the LPGA Sprint tournament. All the traveling across the state was well worth it because Cristie won the Districts, which meant she had won all three of the tournaments that were considered "The Triple Crown" of high school golf in the State of Florida.

After winning the three state tournaments, Cristie suddenly became the subject of numerous articles in newspapers and was followed by photographers. A writer for *Sports Illustrated* even requested an interview for an upcoming issue. With all the publicity and pressure, Cristie missed the cut in the LPGA Sprint by one stroke. Despite the disappointment of missing the cut, Cristie received a tremendous amount of press. Now the name Cristie Kerr was known not only in the State of Florida but also nationally and internationally as she appeared in numerous articles in golf magazines and newspapers. As our family enjoyed adding many new articles to our scrapbook about her emerging golf career, we had several laminated to hang on the walls.

Cristie advanced to the State Finals having to play in the girl's division, where she hoped to bring back a state title. This was a weak field with the exception of two girls who had played in nationally ranked tournaments. Cristie was the first day leader with a super 66, six under par. Everyone felt that this was an automatic victory, but we celebrated too soon. Cristie's triple bogey on the ninth hole was the fatal blow. With a tie at the end of regulation, both girls birdied the first hole of the playoff. On the second playoff hole, Cristie's tee shot went right and after a great recovery shot, she made a bogey; her opponent made par and won. Cristie's bid for the State Championship had to wait another year.

Prior to her senior year, the coaches in the State of Florida banded together to prevent Cristie from playing on the boy's team, even though Sunset High School did not have a girl's team. The coaches claimed that Daryl Baker was not allowing girls to play, specifically because he wanted Cristie on his boy's team. The battle between the coaches, Daryl Baker and the Athletic Director, became very heated.

Somehow the National Organization for Women (NOW) heard what was happening and called me. The members of NOW wanted to become involved, because they felt this situation discriminated against women. Cristie's situation was unique, because she was the only girl in the state playing on a boy's team. Parents of girls who played golf didn't have to deal with the situation caused by her being on the boy's team. While we wanted to help create opportunities for future female athletes, I felt at this particular time in her life, Cristie should concentrate on improving her individual game rather than becoming involved in a political struggle during her senior year.

Sometimes being a controversial figure can impact a professional's ability to receive endorsement agreements with major companies. To avoid publicity which could be detrimental to her future career, our family decided it was best if Cristie did not play on the boy's team during her senior year and instead concentrated on playing in adult women's amateur events and mini-tour professional events, whether for men or women, as an amateur. This strategy was more in line with pursuing a comprehensive plan for the ultimate goal of qualifying for the LPGA. However, I do believe Cristie's courage and determination in being the first girl to play on the boy's golf team opened doors for other female athletes.

Cristie Kerr

CHAPTER TWENTY-FOUR

The USGA Experimental Match Play Tournament 1993

The USGA decided to hold an experimental match play tournament. Most country clubs maintain a handicap system utilizing a computer software program. Players enter their scores into the computer after each round played, and when twenty rounds have been entered, the computer calculates a player's handicap. This handicap is used when two players of different ability play a match in a tournament or just play each other with a small wager. Because this system is self-monitoring, golfers are not prevented from entering scores that are high and forgetting to enter their low rounds, which could lower their handicap.

A higher handicap gives players an advantage over their opponents, because their scores would be adjusted down with the addition of the handicap stroke on a hole. For example: Player A and Player B may play a hole and both score a five, but if Player A received one stroke off his score due to his handicap on that hole, his score would be reduced to a four, thus winning the hole. Players who want to win through this edge on their opponents are referred to as "sandbaggers." It is very hard to beat a "sandbagger" who does not have a true handicap accurately reflecting golfing ability.

A Father's Story

All USGA tournaments are played without assigning a handicap to a player. Usually in match play tournaments, players qualify to advance through a two-day tournament with the field of players being cut to the low sixty-four players. The match play segment of the tournament is played without any handicap. Players either win or lose on their ability, not on a supplemental scoring system. They play against each other with the low score winning.

The USGA wanted to hold a true match play tournament with accurate handicaps. This created the possibility of making this event a national tournament in addition to the events with local match play qualifying at golf courses throughout the United States. For the tournament to be held, a certain number of entrants and special conditions had to prevail. By requiring all entrants to provide their handicap records for the preceding three months, the USGA could try to eliminate bogus handicaps by examining scoring history. The goal was a tournament in which players had true handicaps by eliminating sandbagging to see if a tournament with legitimate handicaps could be played with an expected result.

The format of this tournament was a two-person team with the lowest net score counting on each hole. Net score, also known as a "Best Ball" format, is the score after deducting the handicap. Cristie's partner was Bessie Phillips, who also played national tournaments and was her best friend. Entering as a team, they won the regional qualifier and advanced to the semi-finals. At the semi-finals, Cristie shot 66 at the Country Club of Miami and they advanced to the finals at Lake Nona, held in Orlando, Florida in June.

At the finals the USGA adjusted each of the player's handicaps at the end of each round. By the time Cristie and

Bessie played the finals, they had plus handicaps, which meant that strokes were added to their scores.

Their opponents were two adult women with high handicaps of 12 and 20. While playing unbelievable golf, Cristie and Bessie could not beat the women with the high handicaps. This demonstrated how handicaps are always an advantage when playing in a tournament, because a low handicap player would have to play a round of golf that was nearly flawless to have a chance of winning.

The next Amateur Junior Golf Association event was in Beaufort, South Carolina. On the drive to the tournament, I picked up my dad, Morris Kerr, and brought him with us. Because Dad was starting to show signs of poor health, I wanted him to watch his granddaughter play while he was still able to walk the course. The weather was great, but the course was in sad shape, with the exception of the greens, which were double cut and quick. On the day of the practice round, Cristie shot 67, the low junior score of the day and beat all the pros.

Cristie had a one stroke lead at the end of the first day, and once again Kacie Meyers was on her tail. By the end of the front nine, both Kacie and Cristie shot even (36). By the fifteenth hole, Cristie's lead was three. Kacie birdied the sixteenth, and Cristie bogeyed, so now only one stroke separated them. Another birdie on seventeen by Kacie, and it was all even.

The last hole was a good Par 3, about 162 yards. Kacie's tee shot landed right on line just six feet over the green. Cristie's ball landed some twenty-five feet from the hole. Kacie's putt stopped within one foot of the hole for a sure par. Cristie looked her putt over, and—*BAM!*—into the hole it dropped...HER FIRST AJGA WIN!

A Father's Story

My dad said that I jumped three feet off the ground as I gave out a loud yell, "YEEEEEEESSSSSSSS!" I was so overcome with emotion, especially after seeing her chance of winning the last two events fall apart on the back nine. Best of all, Cristie's grandfather, Morris Kerr, was with us to see this victory.

CHAPTER TWENTY-FIVE
Traveling Increases 1993

Preparing for summer vacation and planning Cristie's summer tour was becoming more complicated. A large map of the United States was spread across our dining room table, and pins identified where the different tournaments would be held. Her mom and I worked on logistics together, choosing the most important events, then working out the details of finding the best motels and methods of travel that were efficient and within our budget. My entire time and budget for vacation was always spent taking Cristie to tournaments to advance her career.

The airplane flight to Jackson, Wyoming for the Women's Amateur Public Links Championship (WAPLC) was long; but the approach to the Jackson area, provided a spectacular view of the Grand Teton Mountain Range. The snow on top of the mountains gave us the feeling that summer had not yet arrived to this majestic location. While the course was flat considering the location, it played a lot longer than the 6200 yards the USGA had set up. Although the greens were fast, the ball held when it hit the greens.

The weather was cold, and on one day we encountered snow, hail storms, rain, and sunny weather. In fact, the weather was so

A Father's Story

bad that I struggled carrying her golf bag into the wind. Finding it nearly impossible to walk forward into the wind, I wondered why the tournament committee did not suspend play due to the tough conditions. Later I learned that those conditions were common for that part of the country, and the local residents paid little attention to the weather and just played golf whenever they could despite less than favorable conditions.

Cristie played well for the two days. She was a co-medalist with scores of 74 both days. On the first day of match play, she played well but lost in the first round to Connie Masterson, who qualified thirty-second and went on to win the championship. Cristie played even par for the sixteen holes, but Connie kept hitting the ball within inches of several Par 3's, and that was the difference between winning and losing.

After returning from Wyoming with one day's rest, we were off to Debary, Florida for the Florida State Junior Championship, our home State Junior Championship. Cristie won by one stroke after playing solid golf for two days. Cristie's name was added to the trophy, which she kept for one year until she returned to defend her title.

Once again Tom Gibson was asked to help Cristie with her putting. From time to time it was necessary to return to the teacher who knew her game best to tweak the part of her game that needed the most improvement. With a little over a week before the next US Open Qualifier in Atlanta, Tom made only minor adjustments to her putting stroke, and Cristie concentrated on putting for that entire week. On the way to US Open Qualifier, we stopped to play the Jones Creek Golf Course. More bad weather greeted us during the tournament, and Cristie missed qualifying by one stroke.

Six players, including Cristie, were in a playoff for alternate spots. By the end of the third playoff hole, Cristie beat three of the five players, including three tour players. By the fourth playoff hole, Cristie had beaten all but one. The fourth hole was 424 yards, a Par 4 that played right into the wind. I knew that this is where the playoff would end. With her length off the tee as a definite advantage, Cristie's great drive hit the green in regulation and won the playoff. While disappointed in the qualifier, she felt better after winning the playoff.

At the Rolex Championship in Marietta, Georgia, Cristie did not play well. When playing well, golfers have a lot of confidence and don't think about the mechanics of the swing. They just pick a target and swing. When Cristie began hitting shots off line, which caused her not to make pars or birdies, all of a sudden she began to look for the cause of the problem. In many cases the only cause was just a bad swing, but when she tried to fix something that was not broken, she risked compounding the problem.

Cristie fell into that trap. Lacking confidence in her swing, she began making small changes which weren't needed. Then when she began to hit shots that were worse than before, her confidence took a nose dive. Many players go through periods like this, and sometimes the only remedy is to take some time away from golf and relax doing something else. Unfortunately, Cristie was committed to tournaments every week, although it may have been better to drop out of a tournament than to continue becoming more and more frustrated.

We flew to West Coast for the next group of tournaments with the first stop in San Diego, California for the Optimist Junior World Tournament. The August weather was in the seventies, a nice break from the hot, humid weather on the East Coast. Cristie shot one over for the four days, which was not good enough to win. Another second place! She did, however, shoot a tournament record of six under on the second day.

A Father's Story

The USGA Junior Girl's Championship was next in Costa Mesa, California, just forty miles south of Los Angeles. The course was magnificent and played over 6100 yards with Par 5's that were reachable in two. By the end of the first day of qualifying, Cristie was tied with Skylee Yamada of Utah. On the second day, Cristie blew the field away with a great 69. Kellee Booth thought that the medalist honor was hers until the scoreboard was corrected, and the 41 that was incorrectly posted for Cristie was changed to 35. Cristie took medalist honors by five strokes but lost to Erica Hiashida in the quarter-finals.

The American Junior Golf Association selected Cristie for the Canon Cup Team, which was a junior golf version of the Ryder Cup. This tournament was a team competition, and it was an honor to be a member of the East Team. On the first day, each team chose four players for the morning round of golf and four for the afternoon match. Different formats were used for each round of golf with the winning team receiving a point for winning the match or a half-point for tying the match at the end of the 18th hole. There were no playoffs in the event of a tie.

The second day brought more team matches, which concluded on the final day with all team members playing individual matches. The team with the most points after three days was the winner. For the past two years, the West Team had made the Cannon Cup competition one-sided, because they usually won. At the end of the first day, it appeared history would repeat itself, but on the second day, trailing by four points, the East girls creamed the West, giving the East a two-point lead going into the last day and the singles competition. Cristie was playing exceptionally well, and during the afternoon match, she played Kellee Booth. The East Team knew that Cristie was the only one who could beat Kellee; and she did, 4 and 2. Even more impressive was that Cristie was five under after six holes. The East Team went on to victory, and Cristie was beginning to be recognized by her peers as one of the best juniors in golf.

We returned to Miami for the Ray Floyd Turnberry Tournament, which was Cristie's first national event after her knee surgery. This time Cristie played steady golf, shooting rounds of 72, 74, and 74. Cristie won by nine strokes. After getting hit in the back with an errant drive during the second day's round, Cristie showed her determination not to quit and to keep going in spite of pain.

CHAPTER TWENTY-SIX

High School Senior Year

The golf season slowed down after summer, and practicing became the focal point. Cristie returned to school as a senior, and I returned to the classroom as a teacher. The next national event was in November in Tucson, Arizona. Without tournaments to keep her interest, Cristie's play during practice wasn't sharp. The typical high school senior girl in Miami at that time was spending a lot of energy focusing on dates and what to wear to school activities such as homecoming, football games and then the prom. Cristie had not been involved in many school activities because she had pursued her number one love: golf. Without tournaments to play and not being on the school golf team, Cristie lacked motivation to keep practicing so that her game would continue to improve.

My role was to find more competitions, nationally ranked events or not, to keep Cristie motivated by the pressure to perform. Finding these tournaments took a lot of telephone calls and research. Although most states had junior golf associations, many had a very limited schedule and usually only accepted residents of that state. At the time Cristie was playing in junior golf, the only national tour was the American Junior Golf

Association, which held tournaments all over the United States, requiring a great amount of travel and expense.

The financial pressure had been enormous on our family. Our resources were nearly exhausted. Credit cards were at the limit; and for the first time, our family was facing the possibility of not being able to send Cristie to as many tournaments. Her mother Linda was willing to sell anything that we had left, including the living room furniture.

I set out to try to find money somewhere, asking everyone we knew, especially family, to lend us money to help her. Not just looking for loans, I hoped that someone would give us the opportunity to follow our dream for Cristie. My mother and sister borrowed money to give us enough for the summer. The money issue continued to be a major concern. While most of the other girls on the national tour came from families with the financial resources to travel and play, we were not in their position. The pressure was getting to us and affecting our marriage.

The next tournament was the Rolex Tournament of Champions in Tucson, Arizona. This time, Cristie made the cut but lost in the second round to Grace Park. Cristie played better in a stroke play tournament rather than match play. We came home to work with yet another teacher, hopefully to get some different ideas on how to win more consistently, especially during match play.

Finding teachers to help Cristie was difficult. Many teachers could help based on their own ability. I was always looking for that one teacher who had the entire package and could take Cristie all the way to the top. I was becoming aware that while these teachers each had their own strength and methods, all seemed to concentrate on the one thing which they thought was the most important, but that thing was not necessarily right for

Cristie. Some teachers were too mechanical, breaking the swing down into too many parts; and some ignored important elements all together. The golf swing and game can become too complicated if teachers don't make adjustments for different physical builds and swings which vary due to muscular strength.

When a new teacher briefly worked with Cristie, it became apparent that her swing was solid, but her ability to excel under pressure was preventing her from winning tournaments. Cristie needed to work with someone who specialized in helping players deal with the mental part of the game. She needed a sports psychologist just as much, or even more at this point, than a golf teacher.

After reading stories in golf magazines about sport psychologists who assisted players facing pressure situations, I was convinced this was necessary for Cristie. At first she was reluctant to accept this as a possible solution because she hadn't read the same articles and was still in the process of maturing. She needed to understand the problem before she would be ready to accept a possible solution. Feeling in complete control of her emotions, she believed she could handle whatever came her way. Convincing her to the contrary was not going to be easy, but I knew that eventually she would entertain the idea and at least give it a try. I hoped it would be soon.

CHAPTER TWENTY-SEVEN

A Special Bracelet 1994

The beginning of the 1994 summer golf season was the Women's Western Championship held in Macon, Georgia. This tournament gave Cristie an opportunity to play against some of the strongest amateurs in the country. While she was eliminated in the third round of match play, Cristie had the lowest two-day score of the juniors who played in this event.

When her score in this event was combined with her score from the Western Junior, Cristie won the Marion Miley Memorial bracelet, which was given to a player to wear for one year, engraved with the names of all the juniors who had won it since 1934. This was quite an honor, particularly when Cristie saw the name Nancy Lopez as one of the winners. Cristie wore the bracelet on special occasions and kept it in a safe place to protect it from getting damaged or lost.

It was time for another try to qualify for the US Women's Open. Most female golfers dream of winning the United States Open because this is considered the most prestigious tournament in the world. Cristie was determined to keep trying to qualify until she had the opportunity to play in this event. The 1994 qualifying event in Haines City, Florida was played on a very wet golf course, as a result of many days of torrential rain. Wet golf courses make playing conditions more difficult. Balls hit off the tee land in the soft fairway and plug into the ground, which shortens the driving distance. This makes the next shot to the green longer than usual and generally more difficult.

In a playoff, one mistake can decide the outcome. After a bogey on the playoff hole, Cristie did not qualify. We packed up and headed home, determined that someday soon she would qualify to play in and win the Women's United States Open Championship. Losing is hard, but Cristie and I kept talking about how well she did in the playoff and how that experience would only help her in the future.

I scheduled Cristie to try to qualify for the Health/South Palm Beach LPGA Classic. This required two qualifiers; the first against only amateurs, with two players advancing to the Monday morning LPGA qualifier. Only two players on Monday would qualify for the tournament. She was even par up to the tenth hole when the torrential rain began. By the time Cristie got to the 15th hole, she was three over. Birdies on 15, 16, and 17 brought her back to even par. On the 18th hole, I felt that a score of 70 or 71 would qualify; but when her forty-foot putt missed the hole by the width of half of a ball, Cristie missed qualifying by one stroke.

This experience made me aware that Cristie needed to learn how to play in bad weather. We began to practice whenever there was bad weather so she would learn how to play with wet grips, limited vision, and nasty conditions. When the rain began, which happens often in Miami summers, we continued to practice or play to give Cristie the opportunity to accept the difficult conditions and focus on playing rather than the weather.

Being able to play in rain requires a player to wear a waterproof rain suit. The jacket and pants, which keep the player dry, are cumbersome and restrict the swing. The player also has to deal with rain hitting her face and glasses, which restricts vision and makes it difficult to see the target areas and execute the shot. The hands and grip are probably affected more than anything else, because the player must be able to grip the club so that it doesn't slip during the swing. This requires the player to have dry towels, which becomes almost impossible without a caddie with spare dry towels in the golf bag. Cristie learned to check what weather was expected at the tournament site so that she could be prepared with the correct equipment and adjust her game to the changing conditions.

CHAPTER TWENTY-EIGHT
Important Wins

The first round of the 1994 Doral/Publix Tournament was canceled due to rain. Several days of rain left large puddles of standing water in the fairways. Just as it appeared this tournament might be cancelled, the rain stopped and the water started to recede into the lakes. The tournament committee decided to shorten the tournament to two days, because so many people had come from all over the world for their kids to compete.

The committee did not want families to leave for fear that they might not return the next year. This tournament was a big moneymaker for Dade Amateur Golf Association with over five hundred kids in all age groups attending. Despite high winds, Cristie won, beating the Rolex Player of the Year. This win inspired Cristie to try harder to gain the distinction of becoming the number one ranked junior amateur in the world.

Golf is not a sport where players can win and rest. There is always another tournament, another title, and more competition to beat. During the winter, the tournaments were held on the weekends because of school. Since the practice rounds were held on Friday, I took a number of days off from my teaching so that we could leave on Thursday after school to travel to these competitions. When Cristie finally got her driver's license, she was able to do some of the driving and reduce the pressure on those long boring rides.

During the school winter breaks, the more important four day tournaments were held. The Doral Tournament was followed by the Junior Orange Bowl, which was scheduled around the New Year's Orange Bowl Football game and parade in Miami. These events generated a lot of interest. In 1994, when Cristie won the Doral Tournament, the Junior Orange Bowl Classic, and the Women's Western Championship, she received tremendous media attention. The newspapers, as well as television channels, all were running spots detailing Cristie's accomplishments.

Having become the "Hometown Hero" from Miami, Florida excited everyone, especially Cristie. She loved the attention, which kept coming at her with increased frequency. As she received more national attention, Cristie could no longer could just show up at tournaments and blend in with the other players. Now in the spotlight, wherever she played, Cristie was becoming a celebrity in the community, especially at school with her peers and teachers. She felt special and enjoyed every minute of the attention. In addition to playing in the tournaments, she was followed by the local media to give interviews before and after the rounds. This added pressure gave Cristie the opportunity to learn how to manage her game with the distractions that came along with becoming a celebrity.

During the month of January, the Harder Hall Women's Invitational in Sebring, Florida brings the best in women's amateur golf together for four days of stroke play. The slow greens at Harder Hall were a surprise to Cristie, but this tournament was successful, because Cristie became a favorite with the fans. With a reputation as one of the best amateur players in the nation, Cristie had developed a fan base from the media attention that she had received over the years. Learning to be more fan-friendly to gain their support, Cristie spoke to the spectators while walking down fairways between shots, and she was smiling a lot, which helped her connect with fans. Cristie won the Harder Hall tournament by two strokes.

As Cristie became more conscious of her image, she selected her outfits for the tournaments to look smart and not attract any negative attention. Knowing that a successful tournament could put her on the cover of local and even national sports publications, Cristie began to pay careful attention to her outfits, hair and overall appearance. I believe the professional but feminine look which she continued to evolve contributed to her marketability for potential sponsors.

Amateurs have to buy their own golf attire. While specialized golf attire is available, many young female golfers just wear shorts and a polo top with a baseball cap. Initially, these girls are not concerned with looking good for the media until they begin to establish a reputation with their golfing ability. At this age most of Cristie's peers who were not involved in competitive sports were spending hours in the malls trying to find the latest fashion to be accepted by their peers.

Wanting to draw positive attention on the golf course, Cristie became conscious of how her physical appearance affected the reaction from the public and the press. The general public appreciates golfing skills, but when combined with a good physical appearance and a fashionable look, the player attracts more attention. Having seen many players develop a unique fashion style, which identifies them from the other golfers, Cristie wanted her choice of clothing to create the right image.

The right combination of colors and style of clothing were important, because Cristie realized this could have a tremendous effect on future endorsements. Advertising is no different in golf than for any other sport or product. Cristie hoped someday to have opportunities with a sponsor to model clothing or accessories. In women's golf, an attractive appearance is important in obtaining corporate endorsements on a national scale. Careful attention to her clothing, weight and overall appearance paid off in later years when Cristie was selected to pose as a sports figure on cereal boxes and to model clothing, watches and jewelry. A celebrity appearance is also important when photographed with national entertainment, sports, political, and financial personalities.

CHAPTER TWENTY-NINE

Major Junior Championship 1994

After a three-hour drive to Winterhaven, Florida, we arrived with great expectations for The Women's Western Junior. This five-round match play tournament had two days of stroke play qualifying the top sixty-four players and then a single elimination match play tournament. Cristie faced a very tough draw when she had to play Beth Bauer in the second match. Cristie won that match on the 18th hole.

Grace Park, the defending champion, was Cristie's next opponent, and Cristie blew her away. The final match was against Erin Kerchevesky from Coco Beach. Erin had always been one of the best "unknown" players in Florida because she didn't play many national events out of town. It appeared Cristie had this match locked up on the 15th hole, until Erin made three birdies out of the remaining four holes. When the match ended at the 18th hole in a tie, Cristie's experience paid off. On the first playoff hole, Erin hit some poor shots, which were her downfall. Cristie made par and won this tournament. This was her first Major National Junior Event—and it was match play!

The Independence Insurance Agent Group Tournament in Austin, Texas was another major stroke play championship.

This promised to be an exciting event, because the hills could take a toll on player's golf skills and physical endurance. Cristie blew away the field with rounds of 70, 68, and 72 and on the final day 65! Seven under par on the last day and a four-day total of thirteen under was her best showing ever. Cristie began to be seen as the "one to beat" because she had demonstrated the ability to fire consistent rounds and shoot under par.

With five days before the PGA MaxFli in West Palm Beach, Florida, Cristie took the next four days off to let a muscle pull heal. Concerned this injury might take more than a week to heal, I advised her not to play. Cristie's determination to compete was so strong that she went on to shoot two over for the four days, but this was not good enough to win.

In the three weeks since the PGA tournament, Cristie's muscle pull was better, but I was worried it wouldn't take much to reinjure it. Cristie had to prepare for three upcoming tournaments, and the best way to prepare was by playing competitive tournaments. The Gold Coast Professional Tour, a small tour in Florida for aspiring young pros, was ideal for helping young golfers sharpen their skills before a big tournament. Cristie played in a two-day event the week before the Doral/Publix Junior Tournament and came in third.

The first round of the Doral/Publix was canceled due to rain. Fortunately, the weather improved so that last two rounds could be played. The most difficult course, called The Blue Monster, was used, since the Gold Course was too wet and unplayable. Cristie shot 72, 72 over the next two days with winds blowing around thirty to forty miles per hour and walked away a winner by five shots over Grace Park, who was the AJGA Rolex Player of the Year.

Our family was disappointed when the American Junior Golf Association did not choose Cristie as the Rolex Player of the

Year. This award is based on the AJGA's criteria. Because Grace Park won two more AJGA events than Cristie, Grace received the award. Although Cristie did not receive this award, she was ranked as the number one junior and woman amateur by *Golfweek Magazine*.

CHAPTER THIRTY

Setting Goals

During Cristie's junior year in high school, she was one of the most sought after golf recruits by Division 1 universities. Numerous college coaches attended every national event. I made a concerted effort to avoid these coaches, because we were not ready to make any commitments or even give reasons why the recruiters should or should not pursue Cristie.

Coaches who were able to corner me wanted to know, "Is Cristie going to turn pro or go to college?" This was the question I was trying to avoid answering. Our family was leaning towards professional golf. If I told the college coaches that Cristie was interested in attending college, each coach would try to sell me on their specific college program. Cristie paid little attention to the coaches or going to college. She was convinced that professional golf was the route she would take and did not want to get into lengthy conversations with coaches and give them false reasons to hope that she would attend their college.

Lela Canon, coach of the University of Miami Women's Golf Team, had been interested in Cristie for many years. Because the University of Miami team practiced at Doral, I saw Lela quite often, and we became good friends. If college were in Cristie's future plans, I was confident that she would have seriously considered the University of Miami.

When Cristie, her mom and I discussed the opportunities for Cristie's future, we carefully considered the options of attending college or turning professional. Most people were advising me that Cristie should go to college for a few years to allow her to mature. I felt that if Cristie went to college, she should stay there for four years and earn a degree. Attending college to play college golf for a few years and not get a degree seemed to serve no purpose.

We set goals for Cristie to accomplish before choosing to play professional golf rather than attend college. As parents, we wanted Cristie to have a realistic opportunity to succeed as a professional at a young age and not just be a "one year wonder" and then fade away. The goals we set with Cristie were to: win the majority of the AJGA tournaments in which she played during her last two years in high school, earn the AJGA Rolex Player of the Year title, win two or three women's amateur tournaments, and win a Futures Tour Professional event as an amateur. I felt these goals were challenging but possible for her to reach. While the competition on the amateur and mini-tour level was good, the LPGA was the toughest in the world. Everyone was a great player on this tour, far better than any Cristie had played against in amateur golf.

These goals, set to a high standard of excellence, were necessary for her to accomplish to have a good chance for success. I specifically wanted these goals to be attainable yet difficult. I knew that life on the professional tour was very difficult. The competition was tough, and the life as a professional involved a tremendous amount of travel and time away from home and family. It can be a very lonely life especially at eighteen years of age when most of the players were at least five to fifteen years older.

Cristie not only accomplished but exceeded these goals and was also named as a member of the 1996 Curtis Cup Team for the United States of America. This is considered to be the highlight of any amateur female player's career. Only ten women are selected every two years to be part of this team, and the selection process is based upon the tournament resume. Cristie was one of the youngest players ever selected to play in this event. While media coverage centered on the veterans, Cristie and some of the younger players earned their share of attention from the media.

A Father's Story

CHAPTER THIRTY-ONE

Return to the Woodlands

In 1995, Cristie played the AJGA Taylor Made Woodlands Tournament for the fourth time and won by two strokes over Jenny Lee. This impressive win was accomplished on the last hole, a 390-yard Par 4 into the wind. Cristie's last shot to the green on the eighteenth hole was from 170 yards. After hitting a five iron into the green, the ball rolled back to the flag on the back of the green, eight paces off the left side. A monstrous bunker guarded most attempts to hit the ball close to the flag. Cristie's shot placed her six feet below the flag, straight uphill. Lee's shot veered to the right, flew over the green, then she chipped the ball onto the green and made a bogey. Cristie drained the putt to make birdie. This tournament was one that Cristie had always wanted to win, and finally, after five attempts, she was the champion.

Now there was one more mountain to climb: the USGA Junior Girl's Championship. Winning this was as important to juniors as the US Open was to the pros, and this summer would be her last attempt at the title. Although playing well, Cristie lost in the quarterfinals.

The next tournament stop was in Tucson, Arizona, May 1995. Arizona's golf courses presented a different challenge than the East Coast courses. Desert, cactus, rocks, undulating greens and blind shots are common to maneuver around during the course of a tournament. An even tougher challenge in the AJGA *Golf for Women Magazine* Championship was The Star Pass Golf Course, where the pros played the Northern Telecom. This was as tough a course as Cristie had seen, with blind shots and treacherous hills, and landing areas on the fairways and greens were extremely narrow. One unlucky bounce, even on the fairway, and a player could make seven, eight or nine. During the tournament, one girl took a sixteen on the 15th hole.

My initial guess was that even par for the three days would win. Was I wrong, when eight over won. Cristie led the tournament at one over at the end of the second day, including a round of 69, to tie the course record, but a nine over 80 took her out of a comfortable lead of four strokes, and she finished second at ten over. While Cristie hit the ball very well, the greens were as hard as a rock and didn't hold.

Learning how to play the "bump and run" shot would be necessary for Cristie to succeed on these hard greens in the future. This type of shot is very common in the United Kingdom. European players grow up learning this shot, because their greens are usually firm. Players from the USA use this type of shot very rarely, but with practice players can learn to make this shot in a relatively short time. The problem is not learning the shot but finding a course where the greens and fairways can mimic European courses. This was almost an impossible task. Most courses in the United States were not like those in Europe, but Cristie practiced the shots needed even though the ball did not react the way it would on a hard, dry European golf course.

The US Women's Open was coming up in July with a one-day qualifier on June 26th. On her way to earning the title of Player of the Year, Cristie needed to win at least two more junior events. We decided that she would play in a greater number of AJGA events than in past years because of the importance of the number of wins in AJGA events when being considered for this honor. This meant additional travel and continued the strain on family finances.

CHAPTER THIRTY-TWO

The Summer Tour 1995

The Woman's Western Golf Tournament and USGA Women's Amateur Championship were the two most important tournaments in the female amateur circuit because the field of players and tournament formats were almost identical. After two practice rounds, two days of stroke play qualifying, and five rounds of match play in six days, Cristie found herself in a thirty-six-hole match against Carol Semple Thompson. Carol was a career amateur with an outstanding golf resume and reputation. Dedicated to amateur golf, Carol had played on numerous Curtis Cup teams.

The first round ended with Cristie up one hole. Cristie and Carol both shot great rounds. Cristie was two under, and Carol was one under. As the match progressed, I visualized Cristie holding that trophy, which would be the greatest win of her young career. The names on that trophy were the history of golf in sterling silver.

With five holes to play, Cristie and Carol were dead even. On three occasions, Carol hit the ball slightly off line and was off the green, but each time Carol chipped the ball into the hole to tie Cristie and move to the last few holes. Finally, Cristie closed out the match with just a few holes left to play. A great victory indeed! Those players and spectators who remained to watch this marathon match were entertained with two players putting on a great display of golf.

A role model for amateur golf, Carol had the talent to turn pro but decided to remain a career amateur. The Western Association Committee members were quite pleased and surprised with the outcome, since Cristie was the youngest player ever to win this tournament in over seventy years. At age seventeen she was the champion of the WWGA Amateur Championship. This was her ticket to the Curtis Cup in June 1996.

The next tournament was the US Open Qualifier. Cristie was exhausted from the nine rounds of golf in six days, and the mental stress had taken its toll, but this is tournament golf. Players have to find ways to unwind and relax, because each week brought a new tournament, and the routine for preparation and play started all over again.

Because Cristie and I were both exhausted, we decided to fly to Orlando rather than make the long drive. After a thirty minute flight, we arrived at the Greenleaf Resort and decided to take a cart and ride around the course with Cristie's notes from last year's qualifier to check out the course layout. This gave us the opportunity to see the course quickly, head to the hotel, rest and get the much needed sleep.

The course was set up exactly like the year before; and after riding around for about an hour, Cristie decided to hit balls, chip and putt instead of sleeping. Just being at the tournament site recharged her batteries. It had rained for a few days before we arrived, so the ground was soft, which was an advantage for Cristie. Her long drives helped her qualify for the US Women's Open with a solid 72.

Immediately, we left for Melbourne, Florida, where Cristie would defend her Florida State Junior Girl's Championship. When she won it for the third year in a row with a solid two under for the two days, the tournament committee, parents and contestants acted as if they knew Cristie would win. We wondered if some players had been intimidated by Cristie's junior and amateur golf record, because when Cristie began playing in national tournaments against players with reputations as the ones to beat, she felt the same way.

The AJGA Las Vegas Founders Tournament was a small event, only an hour away from Colorado Springs and the US Women's Open. We decided that Cristie could play this event as a warm-up for the US Women's Open if she qualified. Cristie blew the field away shooting seven under for the three days, and won by a very big margin. It appeared to me that Cristie had the game to be competitive in the US Women's Open Championship.

We arrived in Colorado Springs three days early. Since I was her caddie for this tournament, we used the extra days get used to the high altitude. At six thousand feet above sea level, the air is much thinner, and most people need about a week to adjust to the change in altitude, where breathing is more rapid and players get tired very quickly. The first day Cristie rested and tried to stay loose hitting soft shots on the driving range. The next day she only played nine holes, trying not to push too hard at first.

The key to winning any Open Championship is to keep the ball in the short grass and below the hole on the green due to the lightning fast greens. A three-foot putt above the hole could roll past the hole and turn into a twenty-foot putt coming back. Additionally, these greens were sloped and very difficult to read or determine what direction the ball would roll. Not only were the greens extremely tough to read and putt, but the grass off the fairway, called the first cut of rough, was almost four inches deep. Any shot that was 150 yards or more to the green from the rough would be almost impossible to get the ball on the green in the right position.

The practice rounds were fun. Cristie played with Grace Park, Kelly Robins, and Lisa Kiggens. Not in the least intimidated by these professionals, Cristie was hoping to be playing against them full time in about a year. While playing well during the first two days of regulation play, a double bogey on the first day and a triple bogey on day two caused her to miss the cut by two strokes. The five greens that she three-putt didn't help either.

This tournament proved to Cristie and me that to win a US Women's Open, the player has to hit the ball in the correct place on every hole. With lightning fast greens and hard ground, Cristie quickly learned the importance of keeping the ball in the fairway. Any shot that came out of the rough would not spin or be able to stop on the green. When Cristie hit the greens from the rough, her ball would roll right off the green into more rough making the next shot very difficult and making pars almost impossible.

As soon as she missed the cut, we left for Chicago for the Western Junior Championship followed by the AJGA Betsy Rawls McDonald's Girl's Championship in Delaware. These were junior tournaments, which did not permit the players to have caddies. Each player had to carry her own bag and make her own decisions with absolutely no help.

Playing with a caddie is easier, since the physical demand of carrying the golf bag is gone and there is someone to discuss the yardage and club selection. When a player is alone, all decisions fall completely on her shoulders as well as having to carry her own bag, which brings the fatigue into play. Now the tournament is not only about making good shots and putting well but also being in great shape to walk and carry a golf bag some five miles each round. Amateur players always carry a lightweight bag that has a built in stand. Most bags with a complete set of clubs can weigh up to twenty-five pounds, without any extra rain suits or towels. Manufacturers make a double strap for the player to put the weight of the bag on both shoulders making it easier to carry.

The previous year Cristie didn't have the opportunity to win The McDonald's, because the last day of the tournament was rained out when she was just a few strokes from the lead. Redemption was the best cure for last year's loss when Cristie scorched the field by eight strokes over the next three days, including a record-setting 64 on day two. At the end of the tournament, Betsy Rawls asked Cristie, "What are you doing to my course?" Betsy was thrilled and excited that the score that Cristie posted was one of the best scores made on this course by any pro or amateur. This was great complement from one of the greatest living female professional golfers.

A Father's Story

CHAPTER THIRTY-THREE

The Rolex Player of the Year 1995

Yes! Cristie was chosen as Rolex Player of the Year! Our entire family looked forward to the awards banquet because this would be one of the highlights in her young life. Cristie spent several days writing her acceptance speech to be sure to identify and thank all of the people who helped her reach this pinnacle of achievement. After the opening acknowledgements, Cristie was introduced with highlights of her accomplishments. Her speech was delivered flawlessly to more than five hundred people who attended the banquet. Cristie's mother, my parents and I were thrilled beyond belief to be present for an honor bestowed on the best junior player in the world and Cristie was it!

Cristie received a beautiful plaque with her name and the title of the award engraved into a gold finished trophy. She had become the one player singled out in junior golf as the best for that year. This honor would be hers forever, no matter what her future in golf would bring. For the immediate future, players would be measured against the record Cristie established. Her name had been etched in prestigious trophies next to some of the greatest players the game has ever known.

Her accomplishments in junior and amateur golf:

1993-1995	American Junior Golf Association (6 *wins*)
1993-1995	Florida State Jr. Girl's Championship (3 *times*)
1994	Jr. Orange Bowl Classic Champion
1994	Doral/Publix Junior Classic Champion
1994	Women's Western Junior Champion
1995	Women's Harder Hall Champion
1995	Women's Western Amateur Champion
1995	Florida State Women's Amateur Champion
1995	South Atlantic Women's Amateur Champion
1995	AJGA Rolex Player of the Year
1996	U.S. Curtis Cup Team Member
1996	Low Amateur U.S. Women's Open

A Father's Story

CHAPTER THIRTY-FOUR

The USGA Women's Open Championship

Pine Needles 1996

The US Women's Open Championship was held at Pine Needles Golf Club in Southern Pines, North Carolina. I had a very good feeling about this tournament, because Cristie's game was solid, and she was ready to play to her potential. This could be the beginning of her move to the professional tour, and this was the second US Women's Open that I caddied for Cristie.

The conditions at the 1996 Open were as tough as the year before in Colorado with the exception of the hills. While the terrain was not as severe, the greens were just as fast. The USGA tournaments are known for having the very long rough, which makes hitting the fairway very important. The difficulty in hitting a ball out of deep rough and getting it to stop on the green is that grass gets between the ball and the face of the club causing the ball not to spin and hold a green. Shots to the green from more than 150 yards in the rough would make a player happy just to make bogey.

Cristie made the cut with room to spare, six over for the two days. She was playing well and the leader, Annika Sorenstam, was just a few under par. The rest of the players were all over par due to the tough playing conditions. Cristie's third-round score of 76 didn't appear to be good enough, but considering that she had to par the last five holes to stay at six over par for the three days, it was a very good score. She missed a lot of fairways with her drives, but her putting was great.

On the last day, we came to the 18th hole, a long Par 4 that was downhill and a dogleg left to the green. Cristie looked at me and said, "Dad, let's show them what I can do!" In contention for the low amateur award, Cristie loved seeing fans lining both sides of the fairway and the bleachers filled to capacity. Her drive was long and left and just rolled into the first cut of rough, which was about two inches deep.

When we got to the ball, we could see just half of it. We discussed the distance; then she selected her pitching wedge and hit it onto the green some thirty feet from the hole. As we walked down the fairway to the last hole, the crowd gave her a great round of applause. As the low amateur, Cristie was experiencing the beginning of a new career.

During her last two years as an amateur, Cristie had received a tremendous amount of media and television coverage. The sports writers and commentators knew the name Cristie Kerr. As she looked over the putt from behind the ball, I looked at it from the opposite side. We discussed the target, and she stepped up to address the ball. The crowd grew dead silent as she hit the putt, and it rolled straight into the cup.

The spectators went crazy! They clapped, cheered and yelled shouts of praise for her that seemed to last an eternity. Tears came to my eyes. I had the privilege not only to see it happen, but I was there, on the green. I still remember the tremendous feeling of pride, joy and jubilation for my daughter, Cristie Kerr! She shot 69 with that birdie on Number 18, which gave her a score of eleven over par for the Women's Open, low amateur and tied the low amateur record. She received a USGA medal for her accomplishment as well as earning her a place in the golf history books. We left the US Open completely satisfied because Cristie knew she could be competitive at this level. Tied for thirty-sixth, she and our entire family looked forward to the next US Open, when she could compete as a professional.

CHAPTER THIRTY-FIVE

The Curtis Cup

When the Curtis Cup selection was announced, Cristie was named to the team. This wonderful news was something our family and the media all expected. The Curtis Cup brought together the ten best players from the United States and the ten best from the United Kingdom and Ireland, the latter were referred to as the European Team. The golf associations from both countries provided each player with uniforms, golf bags, umbrellas and travel cases for golf clubs for this event, all with the logos of the USA or Europe embossed on player's pieces. In team meetings, strategy was discussed, with descriptions of parties to raise the level of excitement among the players. Representing your country is quite an honor, and these players were going to give their all for a victory. During the competition many friendships were formed, which carried into the following tournament seasons.

The USA team coach wanted all of her players to have the opportunity to play an equal amount of times. Because the British coach played her strongest players, the British team had an advantage which led to victory. While winning is the goal of any tournament, both teams gained experience and developed a mutual respect for each other.

Team members from both sides were proud to have been part of this special event. The Curtis Cup team had team strategy meetings and social events to get the players into the spirit of the competition and bond with each other. The parents spent time together, since we had little opportunity to be with our kids on the team. When we weren't following their play, we socialized in the clubhouse having our own bonding parties. Most parents spent time with families that they had bonded with during the golf season. Since many players on the team were older and some were married, the younger players' parents usually stuck together. The food was great, and the hospitality of the Irish was far above what anyone expected. The week spent in Ireland was an experience not easily forgotten.

On the flight back from Ireland, Cristie said, "Dad, I am turning Pro!" This was June 23, 1996, my birthday. This statement was just a formality, because a player really only turns pro when she enters a professional event to play for money; but I was thrilled that she made it official, at least in her mind. Now she would look to a new beginning in her golf career, when she became a professional golfer with the expectation of qualifying for the LPGA.

I felt confident that Cristie was ready to make the transition from amateur to professional golf. In a few months she would turn nineteen, but because she had never known real failure, I expected an adjustment period. What I could not predict was just how long this adjustment would be, but I was confident Cristie would rise to the top as she did in junior and amateur golf.

Cristie Kerr

CHAPTER THIRTY-SIX
Professional Golf

When Cristie qualified for the Health/South LPGA Tournament in Daytona, Florida, I caddied since Cristie was not ready to have a professional caddie carry her bag. Professional caddies want to work for players who provide opportunities for bonus money based on the player's finish in the tournaments. As an unknown, Cristie needed to size up the caddie talent before deciding which caddie would be best for her.

After a good practice round, we talked about each hole including the best club to hit off each tee. Cristie was nervous, because she had been paired with Nancy Lopez during the first round of the tournament. Playing in a professional event as a pro for the first time makes anyone nervous, but playing with one of the living legends of the game is enough to make a normal person feel ill.

The media were all over this pairing on the first day following Nancy Lopez, but Cristie's presence added interest. On the first tee, players introduce themselves and identify the markings on the ball they will be using. Cristie didn't talk much, and just said, "Hi, I'm Cristie Kerr, and I am happy to be playing with you. I am using a Titleist with a red dot."

A Father's Story

That was about all the conversation which took place during the round of golf. Nancy did everything possible during the tournament round to make Cristie feel comfortable. Even though she was there to win the tournament, Nancy made Cristie's experience one to remember for life. At the end of the second day, Cristie was two under par and made the cut. On the final day of the tournament, Cristie did not play as well but finished with the rest of the great players in the field.

The LPGA Shoprite Tournament in Atlantic City, New Jersey was Cristie's first tournament on the LPGA as a professional. Each tournament director can choose any two players, amateur or professional, to play on their exemption. This gives the local tournament an opportunity to invite a local or nationally know player to enhance the field with positive publicity. Most exemptions are given to players whose reputation in golf was beginning to be noticed in the media. Thrilled to be invited, Cristie felt indebted for this opportunity. Being invited to play was great, but now as just one of a hundred and forty-four players, proving her worth was her next big test.

All rookies lack the experience of playing every week and the understanding of how to pace themselves for the entire season. Cristie did not possess the knowledge of the courses which other pros gained from playing many times before. Cristie would face this difficult situation for the next year or two. Not only did she have high expectations, but many articles written about Cristie's amateur record predicted that she would be a superstar right from the beginning. Starting as a rookie playing against seasoned players who were established winners would be difficult enough, but the added pressure of people watching her and waiting for her to fulfill their expectations added more pressure.

Unfortunately, Cristie did not play well and missed the cut by quite a few strokes. She was nervous, intimidated, and tired. As an LPGA rookie, she would play and learn just like she did in junior and amateur golf. Her amateur record didn't scare the pros who had been on the tour for years. Cristie wasn't intimidating even though she was highly touted in the media and the story of the tournament. The veterans, who had seen players come and go before, were not impressed. Their experience was a decided advantage over Cristie.

The professional players had seen girls like Cristie, who had amazing credentials, come year after year and fail to make the grade. Many rookies, who make it to the tour, last only one or two years. If they do not earn enough money to stay on tour, many women become college coaches or teaching pros at country clubs. Cristie's true test would come at the qualifying tournaments in her attempt to earn her exempt card.

The qualifying procedures are straightforward. Two sectional tournaments are held toward the end of the regular season. The top thirty players from each tournament advance to the final qualifying tournament after the end of the regular season. These sixty qualifiers are joined by the tour players who did not finish in the top ninety of the current year's money list and do not have exemptions carried forward from prior years. After the final tournament has played three rounds, the field is cut, and the remaining players compete for exempt, non exempt and conditional status. Status is always determined by the order in which a player finishes in the qualifying tournament for the next year's events.

A fully exempt player from the prior year can play in any event based on the prior year's money list. Only first year exempt players are excluded from limited field events during the next year's schedule. These tournaments generally have only the top thirty to fifty players from the prior year's money list.

Cristie did not win a Future's Tour professional tournament in 1996 and finished no lower than tenth on the six tournaments with three second place finishes in a row. During the first LPGA Sectional Qualifier, Cristie brought her game to another level in Venice, Florida when she shot five under par to share medalist honors with Jenny Lee.

Cristie Kerr

CHAPTER THIRTY-SEVEN
A Full Time Professional

At the end of the school year in June 1996, I took leave from my teaching position for two years so that Cristie and I could travel together full time. Some family members provided much needed capital for us to continue toward the professional tour, paying expenses and also providing some income, since I was not earning a salary on a non-paid leave from the school system.

Not yet nineteen, Cristie was not old enough to rent a car, so I handled the logistics for travel, and her mother managed the money. The expenses which involved travel by air, renting cars, two hotels rooms, food, dry cleaning, laundry, and miscellaneous expenses began to add up. Money which Cristie earned from the Future's Tour was not enough to cover the expenditures, and Cristie had no endorsement contracts at this time.

My unpaid leave from the school system required me to return to work after two years, or my employment would be terminated. When we first went on tour together, I hoped that Cristie might do well enough financially that even if I did not travel with her full time, I might work as Cristie's agent or in

A Father's Story

some other capacity rather than return to teaching. I loved the travel and being involved with the professional golf tour.

Four more tournaments in California on the Players West Professional Tour in California gave Cristie the opportunity to work on her game before playing in the final LPGA qualifying tournament. Visiting the PGA show in Las Vegas provided opportunities to meet some potential sponsors. Unfortunately, most representatives were only interested in talking to the established touring pros. A real benefit occurred when Cristie was invited by the Calloway Golf Company to visit their testing center in Carlsbad, California to test golf clubs so that they could build her a custom set.

Prior to going west, Cristie had signed an agent agreement with International Management Group (IMG) including an agreement for Calloway to pay her $20,000 during the first year on tour in 1997. As the first endorsement for Cristie, the Calloway logo and name was on the side of her golf bag. Cristie began playing with the Calloway brand of clubs, using the Big Bertha driver, the Calloway irons and metal woods. She played with these new clubs before the final tournament in Daytona Beach, Florida on October 22-25, 1996.

Now Cristie was playing for trophies and cash. Playing in the Futures Tour events only required an entrance fee. To play as a member of the LPGA Tour, she would have to play in a sectional qualifier, finish in the top thirty, and finish high enough in the final tournament in Daytona, Florida to earn exempt status for 1997. The number of exempt status positions vary from year to year depending on how players finish on the money list for that year and how many did not qualify for the next year based upon other LPGA qualification rules.

Any player not finishing in the top ninety has to return to the final tournament, along with the sectional winners, to regain their exempt status. The final field for this tournament was around one hundred and fifty players. Those not earning exempt status could earn limited status, or none at all, depending where theses players finished in the tournament. Limited status allows a player to enter only a small number of tournaments the next year. Openings in a tournament are filled when an exempt player decides not to play, then the player highest on the list of non-exempt or conditional players may enter. At the end of the final qualifying, Cristie finished sixth and earned her exempt status for the LPGA year 1997.

CHAPTER THIRTY-EIGHT

National and International Competitions

While waiting until January 1997 to become an exempt member, Cristie was invited to play in two tournaments in Australia. The tournament director wanted to include exempt players in his tournament to increase the number of spectators coming to watch, as well as increasing the appeal of his tournament for sponsors. After a twenty-eight hour trip, we arrived in Melbourne, tired from a six-hour flight to Los Angeles, a twelve-hour flight to Auckland, New Zealand, and a four-hour flight to Melbourne. The last two hours of travel were spent in a rental car trying to find our hotel.

Cristie was excited about playing. A number of LPGA players from the USA as well as Europe would give Cristie an opportunity to play against competition far above the talent level of the mini-tours. In the beautiful hotel, we were treated like royalty. The course was like many in America, pretty flat, with some tricky holes, which required players to hit a very small green surrounded by high rough.

At the professional level, the difference between winning and losing is putting. Jane Crafter, who had a hot putter that week, finished nineteen under par to edge out Laura Davis and Jane

Geddes by one stroke. Cristie finished tied for nineteenth with a four day total of seven under par. She played well but didn't make enough birdies to compete for the top spot. An eagle on the last hole secured Cristie a good finish. We left Australia knowing that some day we would be back to play this course again, because it had become an LPGA tour stop for at least the next five years.

This was the first tournament in which Cristie put together four rounds under par. That gave her back the confidence she seemed to lack after the tournament in Melbourne the week before. Golf can do strange things to your mind. It is the most humbling game that one can play. Just when you think you've mastered it...oops!

When Cristie played in the Florida Open in January 1997 against local pros from Florida, she finished third. While looking forward to the start of the LPGA season, she could not play in the first event, the Tournament of Champions in Weston, because rookies were not eligible. Meanwhile, the tour kept Cristie busy completing the required sixteen hours of rookie volunteer work. Rookies on the tour help in many ways. Sometimes they carry the score placards during a round of golf to give spectators players' scores when the electronic score boards cannot be seen. Rookies also help in the volunteer tent doing odd jobs needed to help stage the tournament, including running errands, getting coffee and donuts, recording data and other miscellaneous tasks.

This work is required of all rookies to give them an appreciation for the volunteers who make tournaments run smoothly and also for the hard work done for the pros to make their stay during the tournament week pleasant and enjoyable. This rookie time demonstrates to the volunteers that the players are receptive to learning about the important jobs behind the scene. In addition, rookies receive an up close and personal look at how the veteran players act and conduct themselves on the course during a tournament.

The Health/South Tournament in Orlando did not go well for Cristie. The weather was cold, and I saw the apprehension in Cristie's face. We were not working together well on the course. After the last round, tired of arguing with her, I threw her bag on the ground and told her I quit as her caddie. Of course, I was still her dad—one role, I would never quit.

After we had come so far, I suddenly had to confront the reality that Cristie had grown up. She had a mind of her own and wanted to make her own decisions. Now she wanted things her way. No longer willing to be guided in her decisions, Cristie was ready to do it on her own, but I resisted. This was very difficult for me to accept. After so many years of being in charge, planning strategies and logistics, suddenly, I was no longer needed. I knew from the beginning that the day would come when she needed to be on her own. The years flew by, and now that day had arrived. I made plans to return in August 1998 to my teaching position in Miami.

Cristie could not play in many of the beginning tournaments because limited field tournaments were based on the 1996 money list. At the beginning of the season, there were two weeks between tournaments in which she could play. It was March before Cristie was able to play each week. Her indoctrination to life on the tour began on the West Coast with the LA Open in Los Angeles, California and then The Cup Noodles Tournament in Hawaii. Playing consistent golf, Cristie shot no higher that par. After Hawaii, Cristie missed the cut in Tucson, Arizona by one stroke. The next tournament in Phoenix, Arizona was a successful outing, where fans started to follow her as they noticed her ability.

Cristie Kerr

CHAPTER THIRTY-NINE
Finding a Good Caddie

Serving as a caddie for Cristie during her early tournaments was a cost saving measure, which also gave me the opportunity to closely observe her game. After a tournament, we would often discuss strategies on the way home and consider ways to improve her game. While I enjoyed the many tournaments I caddied for Cristie, I knew with the arthritis in my knees and my age, a professional caddie would be needed, since I could not keep up with the physical demands indefinitely.

Carrying the golf bag was only one part of my role as a caddie. Like other caddies, I took care of Cristie's equipment, wiping and washing the clubs and insuring the safety of the equipment. Prior to the practice round, I walked the golf course with a yardage book to check the yardage distances. Some caddies use handheld lasers to check distances indicated in these books for accuracy. These yardage books were prepared months in advance of the tournament and sometimes contain errors when changes are made to the course after the yardage book was printed.

By calculating distances, caddies help players choose the correct club for their next shot. By knowing the player's ability, the caddie can decide if the player is choosing the correct club for the shot. When a caddie does not agree with the player's choice of clubs or type of shot, the caddie must communicate this opinion to the player in a way that will help the player rethink her decision and consider an alternative club or shot. This is a difficult position for a caddie. If the player is convinced by the caddie to change clubs or make a different shot and things do not go well, the caddie's future employment could be in jeopardy.

Sometimes caddies have conflicts with players both on and off the course due to personality clashes. Some caddies are excellent golfers themselves, which can be detrimental to the player, because the caddie may forget that the player is making the shot, not the caddie, as the player selects a club or type of shot to make. Caddies' egos may lead them to believe they know more than the player. If the player relies solely on the caddie's advice, the player may end up making bogeys or worse. On the green, some players ask caddies to look over the putt and offer input.

Players should always be in control, listen to the caddie's advice, but ultimately be responsible for making the final decision on club selection and shot. Many caddies have been fired after a round of golf just for giving the player the wrong distance. To avoid these problems, players carry a yardage book and check distances as well as relying on the caddie's advice. A caddie may assume the role of a player's psychologist by helping to keep the player focused and relaxed in a stressful situation. When a player is doing everything right, a caddie is not needed in the same way as when the golfer is playing poorly. Under the pressure of trying to get the player back on track and keep her calm, the caddie has an important role.

The best caddies change players as often as the players

change caddies. Since the caddie's income is directly related to the player's performance, caddies want to work for those players who finish in the top ten. While most caddies for the top ten players earn a comfortable living and travel in style with the player, many caddies struggle to make a livable wage. Expenses are reduced by traveling in groups by car, sharing motel rooms, and eating at inexpensive fast food restaurants. Many caddies earn $30,000 per season and pay for their own travel and food expenses, while a top player's caddie can earn in excess of $100,000 per season and travel in luxury with year-end bonuses as the reward for a great year.

A caddie's weekly salary could range from $400 to $500 with a percentage of the player's earnings after the cut. If Cristie finished in the top ten, her caddie would get seven percent, and a win would give the caddie ten percent. While continuing to caddie for Cristie, I started to interview prospective caddies. Choosing a caddie for Cristie at this point in her career was difficult. The top players had the best caddies, and those who were available had caddied for many different players, being hired and fired as the season progressed for a variety of reasons. Finding a caddie who could work well with Cristie was important.

Caddies became interested in working for Cristie when she demonstrated the potential to become a great player. Her first caddie didn't last very long; and during the first year, Cristie tried several different caddies in her search for a good match. The longer a player and caddie work together, the more caddies learn about the player and her game. The more the caddies learn, the better equipped they are to help the player and not just carry her bag.

CHAPTER FORTY

Frustration Sets In

After the tournament in Phoenix, Cristie was not qualified to play in the Dinah Shore Nabisco, which was a limited field event. We flew to San Francisco to practice before the next tournament in Sacramento, California at the Twelve Bridges Golf Course. Unfortunately, Cristie came down with the flu and had to withdraw. We flew home to prepare for the next group of tournaments to be held on the East Coast beginning with the tournament in Myrtle Beach, South Carolina.

I asked Tom Gibson to come to this tournament early in the week to work with Cristie, but she missed the cut. For the next two months, Cristie did not play well, and her confidence was low. It was hard to stay positive, but her mother and I kept encouraging her. I continued to look for the answer to her poor performance. We changed clubs, talked about strategy, but nothing I did changed the outcome. Her scores were not improving, no matter what she or I tried. The frustration was getting to all of us. We couldn't find a solution to Cristie's problem. To remain on the tour with exempt status, Cristie had to finish in the top ninety of the money list. If this did not happen, she would have to go back to qualifying school to regain her exempt status. Neither she nor I wanted this to happen.

Finally, after two months of trying to figure out the problem, I called Dave Collins in San Francisco for help. Dave Collins worked for Jim McLean as one of his Master Teachers. Because Cristie had worked with Jim in Miami, I was hoping that Dave could figure out what was causing Cristie's poor play. When we found that Dave was available, we flew him to the tournament in Lansing, Michigan to work with Cristie.

Cristie had been hitting the ball all over the course. She and I tried to correct the problem, but everything we tried made the situation worse. After ten minutes of watching her hit practice balls, Dave diagnosed her swing problem, and within a few days, she began to hit the ball better. Just as important, Cristie's confidence began to return. With the caution that the corrections to her swing were not a complete fix, Dave recommended hours of practice to make the corrections feel natural. He also explained that in the meantime she should not expect to hit every shot perfectly. I also felt that Cristie should begin working with a sports psychologist to help her cope with the pressure that she was feeling on the tour.

Cristie had reached a low point for the first time in her career. As an amateur, she always had time to take lessons and fix swing problems; but now that she was a professional, she was always on the road and far from her teachers who knew her swing better than anyone else. As she began to show signs of self-doubt, Cristie became more receptive to my idea about working with a sports psychologist. She was ready to do anything that would make her feel better and play better.

CHAPTER FORTY-ONE

Getting Back on Track

During the next three tournaments, Cristie's scores improved as her decision-making on the course improved. Golfers get into slumps, just like baseball players who keep striking out or not getting on base after a long stretch of playing well. Most of the problem is mental. The player is thinking about too many things at the same time.

When Cristie tried to fix her swing, she tried to correct too many things at once. As a result her swing got worse, not better. Now she was concentrating on only one swing flaw that Dave had corrected. Cristie made fewer mistakes, which led to lower scores during the next few tournaments. As her swing kept improving, she hit a higher percentage of fairways and greens. She was gaining experience, learning how to manage the logistics, prepare and play in tournaments, and deal with the multitude of distractions away from the golf course.

Much of a professional golfer's life is hidden from the public. Fans see players practicing before a tournament, playing a round of golf and signing autographs after the round. In reality, a professional spends a tremendous amount of time planning travel related matters, practicing privately, attending media interviews, and fulfilling required endorsement promotional activities on and off the course.

Many players arrive in a new city the day before playing in the Professional-Amateur tournament. In a Pro-Am, which is usually a five to six hour event, professional golfers play with amateur partners. These events raise millions of dollars for charity as well as giving golfers an opportunity to meet people important to the tour and the tournament. While helping amateurs improve their game, many pros enjoy socializing with these amateurs, who are often executives of companies which may be potential sponsors. A golfer may play with an amateur who is a CEO of a major company and end up with very lucrative endorsement deal in the future.

As a professional, Cristie had reached the point where she needed to be in control of her life and career. I needed to step away and return to my teaching position in Miami. Although Cristie had not reached the levels of income everyone had expected, she was determined to stay on the tour and work diligently toward her goal of being one of the best players on tour. Many pro golfers quit the tour when they run out of money to cover the travel expenses, but Cristie did not have to face that problem for at least another two years due to the financial help from my relatives.

After the first few years on tour, Cristie's earnings kept growing, and endorsement deals started to come her way. She was on the professional tour for six years before winning her first tournament, the Longs Drug Challenge in California. Tears of jubilation ran down her face as she knelt after the last putt dropped into the hole. Her journey had just begun. In 2004, Cristie would win The Shoprite Tournament in Atlantic City, where she made her professional debut, and two more wins in 2004: the LPGA Takefuji Classic and the State Farm Classic.

Her biggest win came in 2007 when she captured the crown jewel of golf, The United States Women's Open at Pine Needles, North Carolina, just ten years after she was low amateur in that event. Since her professional debut in 1997, Cristie has won twelve LPGA tournaments and The United State Women's Open; played on four Solheim Cup Teams; and been honored with the Susan B. Komen Breast Cancer Award.

Professional Accomplishments

LPGA Victories

2002	Longs Drug Challenge
2004	LPGA Takefugi Classic, ShopRite LPGA Classic, State Farm Classic
2005	Michelob ULTRA Open at Kingsmill, Wendy's Championship for Children
2006	Franklin American Mortgage Championship, CN Canadian Women's Open, John Q. Hammons Hotel Classic
2007	**U.S. Women's Open**
2008	Safeway Classic
2009	Michelob ULTRA Open at Kingsmill
2002	The Solheim Cup
2003	The Solheim Cup
2005	The Solheim Cup
2007	The Solheim Cup
2009	The Solheim Cup

Cristie Kerr

EPILOGUE

After I returned to teaching in August 1998, Cristie continued the professional tour on her own. The competition and travel is exhausting, and the pressure to perform constant, but she was determined to succeed and rise to the top. Her dedication and tenacity has paid dividends because she is now an internationally known golf professional. Her wins, top ten finishes, professional earnings, and recognition as one of the best putters have propelled her to a remarkable level. With all of her accomplishments over the past thirteen years, she continues to set higher goals. Her aspirations to be ranked as the number one player in the world and gain entrance into the Hall of Fame are within reach.

Our family is also very proud the tremendous efforts that Cristie has made as a passionate activist to raise awareness and money to find a cure for breast cancer. Her personal contributions, donations made on her website www.birdiesforbreastcancer.com and financial participation by Mutual of Omaha for this cause has raised substantial funds. Cristie founded Birdies for Breast Cancer in 2003 after learning that her mother Linda was diagnosed with this terrible disease. Cristie decided to use her golf and celebrity status to help raise money for research to find a cure. Many fans have joined this effort by visiting the website and pledging a donation for each birdie Cristie makes during the tournament year or making a one-time donation.

Cristie also hosts numerous charity golf and poker tournaments to enhance contributions. Her involvement with this cause has raised her persona as a great player whose charitable efforts are recognized worldwide. Early in 2009, officials from Liberty Health announced the creation of the sixty-eight hundred square foot Cristie Kerr Women's Health Center on the Jersey City Medical Center campus. This facility will offer mammograms, treatment, support groups and recovery services for breast cancer patients.

Over the years, I have shared stories of my adventures with Cristie with my students, interested parents and friends. In writing this book, I have recalled many happy memories and proud moments. I sincerely hope that fans, who have admired Cristie's accomplishments both on and off the course and followed her career, have enjoyed my story. I also hope that this book may be inspirational to other parents and their children.

About the Authors

Michael Kerr's greatest pride was helping his daughter Cristie become a professional golfer on the Ladies Professional Golf Association Tour. In 1965, he was drafted into the Army and deployed to Vietnam for one year. After his honorable discharge, Michael married Linda Mare Lewis and soon Cristie was born. As an elementary teacher in the Miami-Dade County Public Schools, Michael found his teacher's schedule enabled him to devote his free time to helping Cristie learn to play golf and, along with Linda Kerr's assistance, they were able to travel the long, challenging road so that Cristie could become a professional golfer. For more than twelve years, Michael kept a daily journal of Cristie's progress, and it is this book that is a father's story of making a champion.

A professional educator and author, Dr. Barbara W. Moller married Michael in 2000. Having worked as an administrator and teacher for the Miami-Dade County Public Schools, Dr. Moller-Kerr also has been an adjunct professor for the University of Miami, Barry University and Nova Southeastern University. Fascinated with Michael's stories of how Cristie became a professional golfer, Dr. Moller-Kerr wrote with Michael to turn his journal into a story to be shared with friends, family, Cristie's fans, and parents of children, especially girls, who aspire to become professional golfers.

A portion of the proceeds from this book to benefit:

Dade Amateur Golf Association

"The First Tee, a division of the World Golf Foundation, has as its mission to impact the lives of young people around the world by creating affordable and accessible golf facilities to primarily serve those who have not previously had exposure to the game and its positive values. Our goal is to provide the facilities and experiences that will enable kids from every walk of life to partake of a game that teaches values for life and which can be played for a lifetime."

For more information visit:
http://www.FirstTeeMiami.org

Made in the USA
Charleston, SC
16 February 2010